CAFÉ LOGOS   YEAR A
A COMPREHENSIVE AND EXCITING NEW RESOURCE FOR 11-16 YEAR OLDS

PETE TOWNSEND

First published in 2001 by
KEVIN MAYHEW LTD
Buxhall, Stowmarket
Suffolk IP14 3BW
Email: info@kevinmayhewltd.com

0 1 2 3 4 5 6 7 8 9

ISBN 1 84003 782 2
Catalogue No. 1500448

Cover design by Jaquetta Sergeant
Edited and typeset by Elisabeth Bates
Printed and bound in Great Britain

CONTENTS

ACKNOWLEDGEMENTS

To those friends who've provided me with encouragement, laughter and love . . . thanks.

To Liz for her ability to draw blood from a stone and her amazing sense of the absurd . . . thanks.

To everyone who's bought or cadged a copy of *Café Logos* . . . I hope it was worth it! Thanks.

To the other musicians who allow me to jam along and sing the blues . . . thanks.

And to Ruth . . . thanks for everything.

INTRODUCTION

Welcome to Café Logos. Pick a table, sit down and browse the menu. I'm sure that you'll find a mouth-watering selection to choose from and plenty to entertain your sense buds.

The menu is based on the Common Worship Lectionary, Year A. The inspiration for the Café is found in Psalm 34, 'taste and see that the Lord is good' and in 1 Peter 2:1-12, 'a living stone'. The idea is to identify with Jesus as the Living Stone by discussion ('taste and see') and to explore a faith in Jesus through the use of the 'Logos' (God's living message).

Each week is identified as a 'unit'. Units 1-21 are based on the Gospels and explore the life of Jesus. Units 22-28 look at the Epistles and examine the Christian life, while Units 29-33 relate to the Psalms and take a closer look at how being a Christian can affect our daily lives.

All of the main Church calendar events are covered using a 'menu' which is divided into six sections with icons for easy recognition.

TODAY'S SPECIAL: theme and Bible reading for the day.

Nibbles: activities which focus the group on the day's theme.

Tasty bit: an introduction and link to the teaching, using suggestions for worship songs and drama.

Chewy bit: the main teaching session with ideas and guidelines for sharing.

Munchy bit: discussion, thought and focus.

Afters: prayer, reflection and ideas for sharing.

The worship songs are only suggestions. Please feel free to substitute other songs as appropriate. You can use the worship songs as part of group worship or use the lyrics in discussion. All of the worship material can be found in
The source (Kevin Mayhew 1998),
The source new songs (Kevin Mayhew 1999)
The source 2 (Kevin Mayhew 2001)
The American Worship Collection (Kevin Mayhew 2000)

The Australian Worship Collection (Kevin Mayhew 1998)
The Australian Worship Collection Book 2 (Kevin Mayhew 2000)
The British Worship Collection (Kevin Mayhew 2000)
(Many songs from the Worship Collections are also in *The source 2*)

The dramas are intentionally kept short and simple, needing only basic props and two actors. This requires little preparation time and the script can be attached to any convenient surface so that you can fluff lines and ad lib to your heart's content.

Have fun and I hope that you enoy feasting at Café Logos.

TODAY'S SPECIAL

Expect the unexpected!

Matthew 24:36-44: No one knows the day or time

Equipment:
piece of string
sticky tape
paper
pens

As each member of the group arrives, give them a piece of paper and a pen. Ask them to write their name on the paper. As they do this place the piece of string along the length of the room and stick each end down with the tape. Mark one end of the string: 'Dead, buried and that's it' and the other end of the string: 'Journey's end'. Ask the group to consider the question: 'Is death the end of our existence or is there something more?'

After a few moments ask the group to stand somewhere along the string which corresponds with their idea or thoughts of 'life after death'. If any of the group are unsure, which you should stress isn't a problem, then they are to stand somewhere in the middle of the string. If any of the group think there may be an afterlife but aren't certain, then they should stand nearer to 'Journey's end'. And if any of the group think an afterlife is possibly stretching things a bit too far, then they should stand nearer to the 'Dead and buried' end. Once they are all satisfied with their position, then ask them to stick, using the tape, their name onto the string indicating where they stood.

(Allow 10 minutes for this)

There are few certainties in life and, at times, we even question what we thought we were certain about! Have a look at 'Did you feel the mountains tremble?' (*The source*, 80; *The British Worship Collection*, 18) or 'I am walking on the way ahead' (*The Australian Worship Collection*, 26). Alternatively, you might like to use the sketch on page 12.

(Allow 5 minutes for this)

Remind everyone that the group is supposed to be a non-threatening environment and nobody is to think any less of another person because they may have a different perspective than some other group members.

Read Matthew 24:36-44.

If any of us were to say that we weren't just the teeniest bit interested in what the future holds then they've either got life totally sorted and know how to sort out every global problem (answers on a postcard, please) or they're too busy writing their autobiography to care. Life is unreliable. No matter how we look at life or how much we look at the clock and complain about the monotony of our existence, anything, and everything, can change within a split second.

Lots of people spend money and time trying to predict their future and what it holds for them. The question is, does knowing what is going to happen in a few days', months' or even years' time change the way we think and live now?

Just say, for instance, that someone read your palm and said you were going to win a fortune. So, you go and live according to that prediction and use every bit of credit and hire purchase that you can lay your paws on. And . . . the bills arrive quickly followed by a solicitor's letter suggesting that you'd better pay the money back, with mega-large interest, asap. Alternatively, you might decide that if life is so unpredictable and that it could end quite unexpectedly, then you should live life to the full, right now, this instant or even sooner and ignore everyone in the pursuit of pleasure. Pretty soon you've got no friends, no money and no idea how much more of this pleasure trip you can take.

In reality, most of us don't live as if nothing and no one matter. We have people we care for and hope that they care for us. We try and save some money for the future or have an insurance policy as a protection against the unexpected. We are urged to make the most of our future by putting money into a pension scheme just so that we can enjoy our retirement (that is if we aren't too wasted to enjoy it). But the nagging thoughts still continue, 'Is this it?', 'What are we here for?', 'Have I missed the bus?'

As Jesus chats with his disciples, he tells them that at some point he wants to come back. The disciples must have thought he was barking mad but only Jesus knew that his time on earth was limited and the purpose of his human life was soon to be made painfully obvious. Jesus suggests that people will forget or ignore what he's said and done and live as if they weren't accountable to anyone. But, Jesus reminds them, the 'Son of Man' will return when people least expect it. This isn't used as a threat but as a promise that soon evil will become subject to the authority of Heaven, and that Jesus' return will signal the time when the ravages of evil will be put right.

No one knows when all that Jesus said will actually happen. All we do know is to expect the unexpected!

Give each group member another piece of paper and a pen. Ask them to draw a line across the centre of the page and mark where they stand in relation to Jesus. Do they accept and believe what he said or do they think he was just a wise bloke who got on the wrong side of the authorities? Alternatively they may be somewhere in between the two points of view.

Their thoughts and the piece of paper are private and once they have made their mark on the piece of paper they should fold it up and place it in a pocket or somewhere safe.

(Give the group 5 minutes to do this)

Ask the group to be still for a few moments and then read the following prayer:

Lord,
    you know
    that whatever we think,
    whatever we say,
    and whatever we do
    has a consequence.
We are not alone
    and we don't live in a void.
There is a world around us
    filled with hurting, crying, worried and frightened people
    who feel as if their life
    has been squashed, crushed, contorted,
    twisted and bruised.
They don't know what the future holds
    and many don't care
    as long as it looks nothing like their today.
While for some of us,
    life seems to pass by
    in a sort of monotonous grey colour
    with no bright bits
    and very few dark bits.
But whatever we think,
    whatever we know, or think we know,
    you've said
    that the only thing we can depend upon
    is you,
    and that really is an unexpected bonus
    considering that we have such
    a fragile grasp
    on life, the universe and everything.

THE GRANNIES LOOK AHEAD

Characters	Moll and Poll are two weather-beaten females who are acknowledged to be the most formidable duo in the neighbourhood. Their tongues have been known to inflict pain at 100 metres!
Scene	Moll and Poll are standing next to a doorway. Both are dressed in old raincoats, carrying shopping bags and have a headscarf each. Poll has a large bandage around her head — on top of her headscarf.
Props	Two raincoats, shopping bags and headscarves, a bandage.

Moll   *(Busily checking through her shopping bag)* I picked up some real bargains today. As many half-price offers as there were half-awake check-out assistants. *(Has a last quick look in bag then arranges it on her arm)* You know me, never like to miss anything. *(Looks quizzically at Poll's bandaged head)* It looks like you don't like to miss things either!

Poll   *(Gingerly pats bandaged head)* Some things I would prefer to have missed.

Moll   *(Sniffs and looks slightly to one side)* Well, never let it be said that I'd stick my nose into other people's business. If I'm not allowed to know details then I presume it's the end of the matter.

Poll   *(Shrugs her shoulders)* Not a lot to tell. Didn't think you needed to be bothered with trivial detail.

Moll   *(Straightens her shoulders and looks offended)* I pride myself on trivial detail. Malicious comments like that could ruin a reputation that's taken me years to build up.

Poll   Well, I wouldn't want to tarnish a reputation built over years of smouldering gossip.

Moll	*(Nods)* Thank you. One has to take care of the little details.
Poll	*(Grimaces and touches the side of her head)* I wish him indoors would remember to take care of the little details then major headaches wouldn't happen.
Moll	*(Pats Poll's sleeve)* Oh my dear, was it too bad?
Poll	Bad! *(Looks skywards)* I ask you. All I asked was that he pay a little more attention to the house than his pesky aquarium. *(Leans forward)* If I left him to his own devices, he'd sit and stare at the fish tank for hours on end.
Moll	*(Tuts)* Men! Leave them unattended for a moment and they go into idle mode in milliseconds.
Poll	*(Nods)* I wouldn't mind, but he's not had any fish in that tank ever since the accident with the bleach.
Moll	*(Winces)* Nasty one that.
Poll	I gave him clear instructions to clean the tank out. Told him to read the instructions in his fish book while I baked a few scones for coffee morning, and home-made blackcurrant jam.
Moll	*(Winces)* I remember the scones well!
Poll	*(Smiles)* They did turn out rather well, didn't they?
Moll	*(Taps Poll's arm)* The bleach and aquarium incident?
Poll	Oh yes. Well, he said that he needed something strong to remove those stubborn stains.
Moll	Only to be commended. Can't have stains left lying around for everyone to see.
Poll	Course not. *(Looks smug)* I pride myself on having a gleaming toilet.

Moll	*(Rubs her back)* No, no, I agree. Although not allowing anybody to use your convenience isn't the most hospitable way of treating your guests. I can still recall my unfortunate encounter with the bucket at the bottom of the garden.
Poll	It was convenient for everyone. My first attempt at recycling too. Him indoors emptied the bucket around the blackcurrant bush regularly.
Moll	Blackcurrant bush . . . home-made blackcurrant jam?
Poll	Hmm, lovely wasn't it?
Moll	*(Gags slightly)*
Poll	*(Looks concerned)* Are you all right, my dear? *(Pats Moll's arm)* That time of life I suspect. Never mind.
Moll	*(With her hand still partly over her mouth)* Bleach, fish?
Poll	Oh yes. Well, *(shakes her head)* wouldn't it have been obvious that you should take the fish out before you tried to clean them out?
Moll	You have to be behind these men every second of the day.
Poll	*(Touches her head again)* Something I should remember more often.
Moll	*(Points to Poll's head)* And?
Poll	*(Grimaces)* I'd asked him to put that nice decorated plate of my mother's above the door, nice for everyone to see, I thought.
Moll	But you didn't?
Poll	The daft gerbil had only gone and fixed it to the wall with a couple of wedges of wet clay. The clay decided to dry out just as I walked through the doorway.

Moll	And you got a close-up of the plate?
Poll	Didn't see it coming.
Moll	A lot of truth in that statement.
Poll	I know, there's a lot we'd be better off knowing beforehand.
Moll	Particularly what the male species will develop into in later years!
Poll	That'd be nice. Just a brief glimpse of the level of stupidity that they'd attain might have been helpful.
Moll	And what's that icon of stupidity of yours doing now?
Poll	Gluing a plate together.
Moll	Should keep him quiet for a few days.
Poll	*(Pats Moll's arm)* If I'd given him the plate to mend straight-away he'd have cried off with some ailment or other. No, I gave it a couple of days, had the pieces of plate gift-wrapped and gave it to him as an early birthday present.
Moll	How did he take it?
Poll	With both hands and a silly grin over his face. Gave me a momentary suspicious look and asked where the picture was so that he could get the edge pieces in correctly. I told him it was one of those puzzles for the intellectually challenged and he went off humming to the shed.
Moll	Best place for them.
Poll	I agree.
	(Both move off, nodding)

TODAY'S SPECIAL

A fruit and nut case?
Matthew 3:1-12: The preaching of John the Baptist

Equipment:
pen
paper
A3 sheet of paper
different images collected from magazines

Distribute pens and paper to the group. Explain that it is often extremely difficult to understand what some people are trying to say or precisely what they mean. For instance, if someone were to say that they were 'Drouthy', would anyone know what they meant? (Drouthy means to be thirsty.) Ask the group to try and work out what the following words mean and write their *definitions* on the paper:

ASSOT	(Stupid)
MAW-WALLOP	(Badly cooked)
WOWF	(Really stupid)
FRAMPOLD	(Boisterous)
SORNER	(To scrounge)
CURKLING	(To cry)
GELID	(Cold)
GOTCH-GUT	(Fat)
PUKKA	(Genuine)
FUGLE	(To cheat)
FRANGIBLE	(Delicate)
NINNYHAMMER	(Fool)
BRINDIZE	(To drink)
BARRELASS	(To fall)
LOOBY	(Clumsy)

And yes, all of the words are real but not used too often!

Once you've finished reading all of the words ask the group to give some of their definitions before you reveal what the word really means!

(Allow 10 minutes for this activity)

Many things which we read or hear often need a bit of explanation. Why not take a look at 'You're softening my heart' (*The Australian Worship Collection*, 137) or 'I have heard of your fame' (*The Australian Worship Collection*, 30).

(Allow 5 minutes for this)

Ask the group what they thought the lyrics of the chosen song meant.

Read Matthew 3:1-12.
Can you imagine what image John the Baptist would have made? Just think, here's a bloke dressed in a camel-hair suit, a leather strap wrapped around his waist and dipping grasshoppers into a pot of honey and popping them into his mouth! In between mouthfuls he gives the crowd a load of verbal about their antics and suggests they have a lot in common with snakes. He then goes on to give them some tips on gardening and hints that they all could do with a dunk in the river. You can just hear the mutterings of 'Been in the sun too long' or 'What can you expect from someone who wanders around the desert all day?' Quite a few folk would have been making gestures indicating that John was a few grains short of a sand-castle.

John the Baptist was a man who had turned his back on the comforts that most people enjoyed and had given himself to reading and meditating about God. Despite his odd appearance and behaviour, John was recognised as a messenger. His message was that all the people should '. . . Get the road ready for the Lord . . .' (Matthew 3:3). This wasn't such a strange thing to say as you might imagine. During, and before, biblical times the roads were almost non-existent. Those tracks that did exist were in a terrible condition and most people who travelled were warned to sort out all their legal affairs and say goodbye to their family because there was no guarantee that you would get to your intended destination safely.

The few good roads that did exist were built for a special purpose. King Solomon built a road of black basalt (a volcanic rock which often contained crystals). These special roads were constructed to reflect the wealth of the king. These roads were built by the king and mainly for the benefit of the king. They were often referred to as 'The king's highway'. Before the king began his travels a message was sent out telling the people to get the roads repaired and looking good in preparation for the king's arrival.

John's message was just the same, the only difference being that the road to be prepared wasn't made of basalt but of flesh and blood, the human heart and mind. John was preparing the people to hear the words of Jesus and the words wouldn't reach their destination if the 'road' wasn't ready to receive a message from the King.

John was concerned that the people were too occupied with their own comforts and had forgotten who God was! The rulers, politicians and religious leaders were too busy building their own little kingdoms to listen to the message of the 'King'. John was determined that when Jesus began his journey the people had at least been warned of his coming.

Ask the group to spend a few moments thinking about these questions:

- How do we respond to people who are different from us?
- Why do we respond in this way to people who are different?
- Should we all be the same?
- Are we all the same?

Place a large sheet of paper (A3) on the wall. Stick images of different people/cultures/communities/places on to the paper as a collage. It might have more impact if you ask a question and then place an image on to the paper, and continue with question/image until all the images are on the wall.

While the group are still in a quiet or reflective mood, read the following prayer:

Lord,
    I quite like the colour green.
    It reminds me of spring and summer
    and of all those nice bits of the year
    that make me feel OK.
I'm not too keen on blue, purple
    or even pink.
These are the kind of colours that
    remind me of a dodgy trifle
    where all the colours have mixed together
    and formed a right old mess,
    something best eaten with the lights out.
Don't you think people are a bit like that?
All sorts of colours,
    races, ideas, creeds and beliefs
    all mixed together in a cosmopolitan stew.
That kind of mix may be all right for

sociologists, anthropologists and psychologists,
but isn't it a bit much for people like me
to understand
each and every one,
every like, dislike,
idea, taste, culture, tradition and point of view?
I mean, come on,
play fair.
You can't expect me
to understand
what makes everybody tick.
I really haven't got the time for that,
or even the motivation
to stretch my brain
beyond breaking point.
So, if it's OK with you
can I be the one
who's in the right,
does the right thing,
at the right time,
for all the right reasons?
And can I be the only one
who's got the answer,
to what's wrong with the rest of the world?
And can I be the one
who is on the side of justice,
hope and freedom,
standing against hypocrisy,
discrimination and injustice?
'Cos you know that I'm
the way everyone should be,
don't you?
But then again,
I suppose all sorts of people,
all over the place,
could be asking the same thing,
from the same point of view,
thinking that they're
the way
everyone else should be.
Lord,
I think we're all a bit mixed up,
and perhaps it's better this way,
that we're all different,

but the same.
Having the same needs,
hurts, pains, hang-ups,
and longing
to be loved
for who we are,
without judgement,
without prejudice,
without hypocrisy.
I suppose
when I think about it,
I like lots of colours really.
It would be extremely boring
for everything to be the same,
without any shades or texture
to differentiate
between one and the other.
Lord,
thanks that we're not the same
and give me the kind of understanding
that springs from a heart
that wants to be
what you want me to be.

TODAY'S SPECIAL

Who are you, then?
Matthew 11:2-11: John the Baptist

Equipment:
paper
pens

As each member of the group arrives, give them a piece of paper and a pen. Ask each of them to think of all their favourite foods, colours, music and pet/animal. They must not write their name on any part of the paper. Collect all the pieces of paper, shuffle them and then redistribute the paper to the group. In turn, ask one person to read the list on the piece of paper that they have. Nominate one person to try and guess who wrote the lists. Can they guess the author? If not, ask a second person and so on. Allow time for each piece of paper to be read and for one person from the group to try and guess who it is.

You could make it a little competitive by awarding points for each correct guess. Alternatively, have one person read one item from the list and see if anyone can guess the author. Use a scoring system that awards 10 points for a correct guess after one item, 8 after two, 6 after three and so on.

How easy or difficult was it to guess who wrote the lists? How well does each member of the group know the other members?

(Allow 10 minutes for this activity)

Getting to know someone takes time. The process isn't always easy and often needs us to persevere.

Have a look at 'You pulled me up when I was down' (*The Australian Worship Collection*, 134) or 'What a friend I've found' (*The source*, 565).

(Allow 5 minutes for this)

How do we really get to know people? What are the good things about making friends? Why is it sometimes difficult to make friends?

Read Matthew 11:2-11.
John the Baptist was in prison (he'd got on the wrong side of Herodias, who was the wife of Herod and had previously been the wife of Herod's

brother Philip, but that's another story). John had heard a great deal about Jesus and what he was saying. His curiosity aroused, John sent some of his followers to find out who exactly Jesus was. In fact, John told his followers to ask Jesus whether he was the one who they were looking for or were they to expect someone else.

Can you imagine a couple of guys going up to another guy and saying 'Are you the one we're supposed to be looking for or not? 'Cos if not, then we're to look for some other geezer.' This wasn't really meant to sound crazy, it just sounded like it! The problem was that John was expecting the Christ to come and act like a judge, telling people what they'd done wrong and what would happen to them if they continued behaving that way (Jesus did say words to this effect later on). So when John heard what Jesus was saying and doing, it confused him a little bit.

Jesus' reply to the odd question simply reminded John of some predictions from the Old Testament.

Isaiah 29:18-19
The deaf will be able to hear whatever is read to them; the blind will be freed from a life of darkness. The poor and the needy will celebrate and shout because of the Lord, the Holy God of Israel.

and

Isaiah 61:1
The Spirit of the Lord God has taken control of me! The Lord has chosen and sent me to tell the oppressed the good news, to heal the broken-hearted, and to announce freedom for prisoners and captives.

Jesus wanted John to know that what God had promised would happen was now happening.

John wasn't accused of doubting or lacking faith in God. All Jesus wanted to do was to open John's eyes to everything that God wanted to do. No one expected John, or anybody else, to immediately recognise who Jesus was and what he had come to say and do. Unfortunately, John had difficulty seeing and hearing much more about Jesus, Herod cut his head off! Fortunately, the disciples and the rest of the population of Israel had a bit more time to get to know Jesus.

For us, getting to know Jesus isn't a snap of the fingers and we know it all and more. Getting to know Jesus is all about a relationship, one which takes time to grow. A lot of the relationship is simply taking the time to chat and experience the day-to-day with Jesus. Another aspect of the relationship is getting to know Jesus through the Bible and accepting that exactly what he said is exactly what he will do. It all takes time but there again, time is all it takes. In other words, enjoy the experience of getting to know Jesus and don't give yourself a headache purely because it doesn't happen overnight.

Give everyone a piece of paper and a pen. Explain that they are going to ask God a question. Suggest to each member of the group that they think about a situation or issue that they find difficult or confusing. Ask them to write one situation or issue on the paper and finish it with: 'And so what would you do, God?'

Collect the pieces of paper and tell the group that you will try to find answers, using the Bible, that reflect something of the character of God.

(Allow 5 minutes for this)

Ask the group to be quiet for a few moments and consider what it might mean to experience God getting involved in their lives. While everyone is quiet, read the following:

Psalm 36:5-7
Your love is faithful, Lord,
   and even the clouds in the sky can depend on you.
Your decisions are always fair.
They are firm like mountains, deep like the sea,
   and all people and animals are under your care.
Your love is a treasure,
   and everyone finds shelter in the shadow of your wings.

TODAY'S SPECIAL   **What a dream!**
Matthew 1:18-25: The birth of Jesus

Equipment:
paper
pens

Distribute a pen and paper to everyone in the group. Ask them to think about an odd or strange dream that they've had recently (you may have to verbally edit some dreams!). Tell them to write one sentence at the top of the paper and then fold the top of the paper over so that the writing cannot be seen. They should then pass the paper to the person on their left and then, once everyone has exchanged papers, they write a second sentence about their dream. Continue to fold the paper over after each added sentence and exchange papers until the written accounts of their dreams have finished (this may take a bit of co-ordination as not all dreams will be of the same length). Ask the group to exchange papers one more time and then each member of the group should read the dream story that appears on the piece of paper. The result should be a little bit weird!

(Allow 10 minutes for this activity)

It may be a cliché, but different things do mean different things to different people. God can speak to us using words, ideas or situations so that he can communicate with us in a way we can understand and appreciate.

Have a look at 'We will seek you first' (*The American Worship Collection*, 98) or 'We lift our voices' (*The American Worship Collection*, 94).
(Allow 5 minutes)

We all have dreams of one sort or another. Sometimes those dreams are extremely vivid and we remember them throughout the day. Other times, we can hardly remember anything about the dream but we are left with a curious feeling, not quite being able to explain why we feel this way but, somehow our subconscious decided to delve into the far reaches of our mind and project thoughts and images onto our cinematic sleep-time.

Read Matthew 1:18-25.

Joseph had a dream . . . a great, stonking, technicolour, 3-D, front row sort. Imagine, here's a bloke who's just found out that the woman he was engaged to is pregnant! You know how it is, take it in your stride, no problem, happens every day. Wrong!

The Jewish tradition was for the marriage to be taken in three stages. Firstly, an engagement was often announced while the couple were still children, their engagement having been arranged by the children's parents. Second was the 'betrothal'. This was the official bit which lasted a year and could only be called off if the female was unwilling to go ahead before the formal agreement had been announced. To break off the 'betrothal' was only possible by divorce. The third part was the actual marriage ceremony, which occurred at the end of the year of betrothal.

Tradition had ruled that if a woman was pregnant before marriage then she was considered to be promiscuous and could, after a public trial, be stoned to death. Fortunately, at the time of Mary and Joseph's betrothal, stoning had become history (to a large cheer of relief from a percentage of the female population). It was now custom to conduct a 'secret' divorce and keep the problem as far from wagging tongues as possible. This was the action that Joseph had decided upon before the dream.

So, there he goes, off to bed with a cluttered head full of angry thoughts and feelings of rejection. Then, just as soon as his eyelids hit the cheeks, along comes a gold-framed dream direct from God. Can you imagine, God tells him that it's still OK to marry Mary, she may be pregnant but she hadn't been unfaithful to him and she was still a virgin! Having received all of this, Joseph turned over and carried on snoozing . . . no he didn't! Joseph listened to what he'd heard and did exactly as God had asked him to. He married Mary even though a lot of people would have suggested that he hadn't been able to wait until his marriage before starting a family or that he'd failed to follow customs of the Jewish law and walked in the opposite direction to Mary.

Joseph heard God, did as he was asked and kept faith in God's word. God had used a dream to get through to Joseph and the dream had packed a real punch. Joseph was to remember that dream many times during Mary's pregnancy and afterwards.

Is it possible that we too can hear from God, do exactly as he asks and stick with it even when the gossip suggests that we may be a few biscuits short of a packet? A few years ago, before crossing the road, children were encouraged to 'Stop! Look! And Listen!' Not a bad piece of advice especially when God wants to have a word in our ear.

Dreams often feature ours fears, hurts, hopes or a mixture of all three! Ask the group if any of them would be willing to share with everyone an ambition or hope which they have. It may be that someone is hoping to pass their exams and continue their studies but are afraid of failing; it might be that someone feels hurt at being left out of an event that they were looking forward to being a part of. Whatever it may be, you can use this time to encourage that person and maybe offer to help, pray for or just be someone who'll listen to the hassles.

Also, use part of this time to answer one of the questions that one of the group raised last time.

Ask the group to be quiet for a few moments while you read the following prayer:

Lord,
   it's quite a crazy thought
   that somewhere
   in the technicolour maze
   of my dreams, that somehow, somewhere,
   you might want to have a word with me!
I think I'm a bit embarrassed really.
My dreams are what you might call
   a visual dustbin,
   a montage of funny bits, dodgy bits,
   gruesome bits and just plain wacky bits.
I have other dreams of course.
The sort where I want to do
   all kinds of exciting things,
   go to exciting places,
   meet loads of different people
   and immediately forget their names.
There's so much I want to do
   but I'd sort of
   want your opinion on things.
So if you don't mind,
   can we talk about it,
   think about it
   and even dream about it?
'Cos I'm not so sure
   that I can get through this on my own.
Be with me, Lord,
   guide my ways
   and help me through
   whatever comes my way.

TODAY'S SPECIAL

All in a dream

Matthew 2:13-23: The escape to Egypt

Equipment:
postcards
paper
pens
envelope
music and lyrics

Write statement one (below) on the first postcard, statement two on the second postcard and so on until all the statements have been written on postcards (you might like to add some of your own statements too).

1. Over 2500 left-handed people are killed each year in the USA, from using products made for right-handed people.
2. If you were to count for 24 hours a day, it would take 31,688 years to reach one trillion.
3. A crocodile always grows new teeth to replace the old teeth.
4. The sentence: 'The quick brown fox jumps over the lazy dog,' uses every letter of the alphabet.
5. The only fifteen-letter word that can be spelt without repeating a letter is 'Uncopyrightable'.
6. A hedgehog's heart beats 300 times a minute on average.
7. Camels have three eyelids to protect themselves from sand blowing into their eyes.
8. Ancient Egyptians slept on pillows made of stone.
9. Around 1000 BC, most Egyptians were dead before their thirtieth birthday.
10. Every time you lick a stamp you are consuming one tenth of a calorie.

Give each member of the group a piece of paper and a pen. Distribute the cards, one to each member of the group, and ask them to read the statement on the card. They then ask the rest of the group whether they think the statement is true or false. After each statement each group member writes their answer on the piece of paper. Once all the statements have been read you can reveal that they are all true. Total the scores and see who has the most correct answers.

(Allow 10 minutes for this activity)

Behaving in the way that we feel God is asking us to requires a lot of courage. If anybody tells you it's easy you have permission to ignore them!

Try looking at 'I trust in you, my faithful Lord' (*The source 2*, 804) or 'Come, now is the time to worship' (*The source 2*, 662). Alternatively, you might like to use the sketch on page 30.

(Allow 5 minutes for this)

Ask the group what they thought of the lyrics to the chosen song. What point were the lyrics trying to make?

Read Matthew 2:13-23.
No sooner had Joseph started to get his head around the idea of a pregnant girlfriend than three wise men turn up with gifts that weren't cuddly, couldn't feed the baby, and certainly wouldn't treat nappy rash!

At some stage Joseph must have dreamt of a normal, traditional betrothal, a nice wedding where aunties cried while uncles drank the wine, and the beginning of a marriage where lots of people gave them gifts and threw confetti . . . or rice, or dates, or orange pips or something. But God had other ideas for Joseph and his bride.

God had already spoken to Joseph in a dream to assure him that Mary was faithful and that the child she would eventually give birth to was special. Now, after using a dream to warn the wise men to make a detour on the way home, God speaks to Joseph again through a dream. So, Joseph and his new family take a long holiday in Egypt, where Joseph has another dream (quite a while later) telling him to go home to Israel then another dream telling them to go and live in Nazareth!

The Bible doesn't tell us whether Joseph had a habit of eating vast quantities of cheese before he went to bed but he certainly had some vivid dreams! But, the most important point is that Joseph was obedient to what he felt God was telling him to do. Even though Joseph would almost certainly have felt fazed, anxious, frightened and a few fries short of a happy meal, he still placed his trust in God. Each time he listened and obeyed God Joseph was building his confidence in what God said and did. Often Joseph wouldn't have a clue what God was up to; he still went ahead and built his faith in God each step of the way. There would have been a lot of criticism and pointing fingers but Joseph was learning to trust in a God who kept his promises.

Use this opportunity to answer another of the group's questions from Unit 3.

If there is time, ask the group what things or actions they feel unable to trust God with. Suggest that the group write their answers on a piece of paper, fold them up and place them in an envelope.

Put the envelope in the centre of the room and ask the group to be quiet for a few moments while you read the following Psalm.

Psalm 37:4-8, 23-24
Do what the Lord wants,
    and he will give you your heart's desire.
Let the Lord lead you and trust him to help.
Then it will be as clear as the noonday sun that you were right.
Be patient and trust the Lord.
Don't let it bother you when all goes well for those who do sinful things.
Don't be angry or furious. Anger leads to sin . . .
If you do what the Lord wants,
    he will make certain each step you take is sure.
The Lord will hold your hand,
    and if you stumble, you still won't fall.

THE GRANNIES DREAM

Characters   Moll and Poll, the two aged icons of femininity, whose reputation is as feared as their tongue.

Scene   Both seated on a settee supping tea and biscuits.

Props   Tea and biscuits, settee, large furry slippers and aprons.

Poll   *(Stretches out her feet, admiring her furry slippers)* Bargain, these were.

Moll   They'd have to be to get someone to buy them. *(Stretches out her own furry slippers)* Full price.

Poll   *(Shocked)* You paid full price! But you never pay full price for anything.

Moll   *(Takes a sip of tea)* Sometimes even I make an exception when you come across something that is as well made and classy as these slippers are.

Poll   *(Shudders)* The stuff of nightmares.

Moll   *(Angrily)* Nothing of the sort!

Poll   They were in my dream.

Moll   It's only in your dreams that you'd be able to afford something quite as exclusive as these.

Poll   Still gave me nightmares. *(Sips tea and then takes a bite of her biscuit)*

Moll   What are you on about?

Poll   Nightmares.

Moll	*(Sips tea)* Sleeping next to that lump in bed is enough to give anyone a nightmare.
Poll	I'll have you know I bought a new mattress only last month.
Moll	Still got the lump, though?
Poll	*(Nods)* Tried to offer him in part-exchange but the salesman wouldn't have any of it.
Moll	It wasn't that long ago that you could trade in anything. Nowadays these fancy shops have fancy ideas.
Poll	I told them he'd make an excellent exhibit. They could place him on any bed and he wouldn't move for days.
Moll	*(Nods and sips tea)* Him and mine together would make a good pair. If gravity didn't make such a demand on their vertical posture, they'd make a fine pair of organic bookends.
Poll	*(Smiles)* How about painting them both white and putting them in a gallery as living sculptures?
Moll	Nice idea, but I doubt you'd get away with it. Trading standards you know.
Poll	I suppose you're right. There must be some law against it.
Moll	Yes, you're right. We'd never get away with calling them *living* sculpture. Neither of them moves enough to justify the title.
Poll	*(Shakes her head)* You have to say one thing for them, though.
Moll	What's that?
Poll	Neither of them moves fast enough to create any dust.
Moll	*(Nods)* You've got to give them that.
Poll	Although I wouldn't say no to a nice, fast-moving young hulk.

Moll	In your dreams, girl.
Poll	*(Shudders)* That's the problem at the moment.
Moll	What, concerned about your mature looks?
Poll	No, my dreams.
Moll	Nothing wrong with having dreams. You've got to have something to look forward to.
Poll	Not *my* dreams. They've been giving me a lot of bother recently.
Moll	Changed your diet?
Poll	Not that you'd notice.
Moll	Well, in my experience, a change in diet can usually be held accountable for most things.
Poll	*(Sips tea)* As in?
Moll	*(Takes a sip of her tea)* Strange behaviour.
Poll	*(Nods)* Now, that I can understand.
Moll	You can tell a lot from diet.
Poll	Especially in the podgy stakes!
Moll	Besides that. For instance, you know when him indoors begins to refuse a fourth helping of pudding that he's noticed a new female has begun working at the fruit store.
Poll	*(Bites her biscuit)* Mine wouldn't eat his potatoes for days until I pointed out that the new woman at the donkey rental was on her fifth husband. All the others disappeared in mysterious circumstances!
Moll	I bet that stopped him dreaming!

Poll	Asked for a triple helping of mashed potatoes the very same night.
Moll	That's the way. Now, what's this about dreams yourself?
Poll	*(Places cup and saucer gently on her lap)* I've had such realistic dreams recently. They've lingered in my head for hours afterwards.
Moll	Are they about anything in particular?
Poll	Well, sort of. They seem to take everyday, ordinary events and create weird things.
Moll	That's marriage for you!
Poll	No, I mean my dreams have taken people I know and places I recently visited and mixed them up to make a sort of surreal story-line.
Moll	Doesn't mean a thing. Just your imagination having fun at the expense of reality.
Poll	You sure that there's nothing to worry about. I mean, aren't some dreams meant to mean something?
Moll	*(Takes another sip of tea)* Take my advice, leave off that peculiar cheese you often indulge in, eat less pickled gherkins in bed and, *(pats Poll's arm)* take my word for it, leave the fish paste for sandwiches. There's absolutely no truth in the rumour that it helps prevent wrinkles.
Poll	I'm glad to hear it. It makes an awful mess on the pillowcases.
Moll	I'm sure that these dreams will soon pass as the dawn approaches.
Poll	That's reassuring.
	(Both Poll and Moll sip their tea)

TODAY'S SPECIAL   **This planet earth . . .**
John 1:1-9, 10-18: The Word of life

Equipment:
card
paper
pens
candles
match
music and lyrics

Listed below are all the major planets of our own sun. Firstly, the planets' names have been rearranged and, secondly, they are not in order according to distance. Each group member needs to unravel the planet's name and then list them in order of distance beginning with the nearest to the sun and furthest away from the sun.

1. Heart
2. Rams
3. Curry me
4. Nuves
5. Nutars
6. Lutop
7. Teen pun
8. Tierupj
9. Suruna

The correct order should be Mercury, Venus, Earth, Mars, Jupiter, Saturn. Uranus, Neptune, Pluto.

Distribute the paper and pens to the group and ask them to solve the planetary problem!

(Allow 10 minutes for this)

It might not have been difficult to work out the jumbled letters of the planets but placing them in order of distance was, most probably, all guesswork!

Take a look at 'You laid aside your majesty' (*The source*, 601) or 'All heaven declares' (*The source*, 8).

(Allow 5 minutes for this).

Take a look at the lyrics to your chosen song. What do they say about God?

Read John 1:1-9,10-18.
The whole solar system is so vast that even if we could map every single part of it the sheer complexity and variety would be virtually impossible to comprehend. It is all so awesome that rather than try and understand every minute detail it's easier just to simply stare at its beauty.

If you look at the night sky, the planets and stars, your senses are overwhelmed. Words fail to describe fully the vision before you. That's something like John the Baptist would have felt when he saw Jesus. Here was God's promise to humankind, in the flesh and offering one blessing after another (see verse 16). Just as the sun provides light and life for the earth, it shines on every one of us and even lights up the other planets without losing any of its brightness. Again, here was Jesus offering God's love and blessing to everyone irrespective of who or where they were. This 'grace', or undeserved kindness from God, is endless. It knows no limits or boundaries. It has no preferences or priorities. God's grace is constant and timeless with a beauty that defies explanation. Rather than read a library full of books about the subject, why not simply experience all that God has for us? God wants the best for us today, tomorrow and the days after that. His love for us is constant and there's nothing we can do to make us feel that we deserve it. It's a simple fact, God loves us and wants us to experience life to the max. God wants nothing but the best for us. Isn't it easier to place our trust in the creator of such a vast solar system than put our faith in what we see and understand?

Give every member of the group a candle. Light your candle and then light the candle of the person sitting next to you. They, in turn, light the candle of the person sitting next to them and so on until every candle has been lit. Ask the group to focus on the candle flame. Explain that just as one candle can light another, so can God's love be passed on to those we meet from day to day.

(Allow 5 minutes for this)

While the group are still holding their candles, read the following prayer:

Lord,
  although I want to understand so much,
  and be able to explain everything that I learn,
  I can't help feeling that it's just not possible
  to put everything into words,
  or reduce what we see and experience
  into a formula or rule.
Some things are just awesome,
  without boundaries,
  without limits
  and are best left
  for the eye and heart to soak in their beauty.
Just as the sun shines on everyone
  without us waking up each day
  and reading a scientific textbook
  or listening to some long-winded debate
  about why and how,
  we accept the fact that it's there.
Surely that's a bit like your love for us?
We really don't need to understand
  every little detail to appreciate it.
  it's simply there,
  for me,
  for them,
  for everyone.
And I think that's totally awesome.

TODAY'S SPECIAL	**Wise up!** Matthew 2:1-12: The wise men

Equipment:
sticky labels
pen and paper for each person
music and lyrics

Before the group arrive write the following words onto the sticky labels:

Friday	Christmas	Father	Baby
Deer	Old	Uncle	Auntie
Computer	Mug	Tree	Paper
Sweet	Sour	Pie	Custard

You can add more items to suit the number of the group. As the group arrive stick one of the labels on their backs, but don't tell them what it is. Tell everyone to move around and ask other members of the group, 'What is my label?' The other group members have to mime the item and can only answer yes or no to questions. When someone has guessed correctly what their label is they can sit down and watch the others trying to guess theirs.

(Allow 10 minutes for this activity)

It can be extremely frustrating knowing that the answer to your dilemma is literally behind you but you have to depend on other people to tell you what it is.

Have a look at 'We will glorify' (*The American Worship Collection*, 97) or 'With our hearts' (*The American Worship Collection*, 103).

(Allow 5 minutes for this)

Take a look at the lyrics to the song and ask the group if the words meant anything to them.

Read Matthew 2:1-12.
When people buy presents for us they usually have a good idea of our likes and dislikes, favourite music, clothes and current rave chocolate

bar. The choice of present isn't just a random 'pick anything off the shelf and hope it's OK' type of thing. Presents are given with the hope that the recipient will appreciate (and possibly really like) the choice of gift which will earn the buyer a heartfelt 'thank you'. More often than not, we can even guess what certain people will buy or give us as a present. You know, Gran always buys you a book token equivalent to the price of a book in 1920 while Uncle Arthur never fails to give you a crumpled paper bag containing a selection of boiled sweets. And, on a good year, Great Aunt Dot will give you a box of patterned handkerchiefs which she received for Christmas two years ago.

Often the selection of a present has been given lots of thought and chosen to 'fit' the recipient. Usually a present means something, even if it is only a 'Look, I remembered!'

The wise men didn't just happen to be passing the stable where the infant Jesus was. Neither did they hear about his birth and rush down to the nearest shop and pull any old thing off the shelf. Each present was given for a reason, to mean something, to reflect something of the character of the recipient.

Gold has always, and still does, represent royalty. In Old Testament times it was also a sign of holiness.

Frankincense was a very desirable perfume. It was used by the Jewish priests in the Temple who acted as the 'middle-men' between God and the people.

Myrrh was another perfume used to relieve pain and to anoint the dead prior to burial.

Each of the wise men's gifts represented something of the character of Jesus. He was a Holy King who would act as the bridge-builder between God and the people and would eventually suffer and die as a sacrifice.

The wise men had travelled a great distance to bring their gifts. They knew something of the character of the infant and each gift had a particular significance.

For each of us, Jesus himself became a gift. He became the once and for all sacrifice that would enable us to form an eternal relationship with God. Now, that's a gift that really means something!

Give each member of the group a piece of paper and a pen. Chat about what everyone thinks would be the ideal, totally most awesome present. After that, ask everyone to imagine that they are a present which is going to be given to someone they respect, love or admire. What kind of present would they be? Ask them to write their idea onto their piece of paper. Secondly, get everyone to think about what gift they would be if they wanted to make a difference in somebody's life. For example, if they wanted to make a difference to the life of someone who was physically unable to leave their home, they might like to be a car so that they could transport the housebound person wherever they wanted to go. Write the second idea down onto the piece of paper. Compare the two ideas. How different are they? When we are buying a present does it make a difference whether we know the people very well or not?

Suggest to the group that it would be a good idea to be quiet for a few moments and to think what they could do to help people who are in need of some care and attention. While the group are quiet read the following Psalm:

Psalm 107:1-9, 43
Shout praises to the Lord!
He is good to us, and his love never fails.
Everyone the Lord has rescued from trouble should praise him,
    everyone he has brought from the east and the west,
    the north and the south.
Some of you were lost in the scorching desert, far from a town.
You were hungry and thirsty and about to give up.
You were in serious trouble,
    but you prayed to the Lord, and he rescued you.
Straight away he brought you to a town.
You should praise the Lord for his love
    and for the wonderful things he does for all of us.
To everyone who is thirsty, he gives something to drink;
    to everyone who is hungry, he gives good things to eat . . .
Be wise! Remember this and think about the kindness of the Lord.

TODAY'S SPECIAL   **To the power of Three!**
Matthew 3:13-17: The baptism of Jesus

Equipment:
paper/plastic straws
string
table tennis balls
sticky tape
pens
paper
music and lyrics

Divide the group into small teams. Give each team eight straws, sticky tape, one metre of string and a table tennis ball. The objective for each team is to build a structure which will transport the table tennis ball one metre along the string without any form of propulsion other than gravity.

The easiest solution is to build two tripods (using three straws in each!) with one tripod higher than the other. Stretch the string between the two tripods and make a carriage from the remaining two straws for the table tennis ball.

(Allow 10 minutes for this activity)

Working as a team is never an easy thing to do. Why not have a look at: 'Holy Spirit rain down.' (*The source 2*, 745) or 'Jesus, Jesus you are the one.' (*The Australian Worship Collection Book 2*, 55).

(Allow 5 minutes for this)

Ask the group if they thought the lyrics developed a particular theme or idea.

Read Matthew 3:13-17.
The baptism of Jesus is a remarkable episode in the New Testament. The scene of Jesus' plunge into the waters of the River Jordan and John the Baptist's claim that it should be Jesus baptising John are often used to pinpoint the start of Jesus' introduction to the general public. However, an often overlooked part of this whole episode is the fact that it is at the River Jordan that the three characters of God are displayed. Firstly,

Jesus showed everybody that the first step towards a relationship with God the Father was in repentance through baptism (water being a sign of purification). The second stage was the appearance of a dove as a sign of purity and graciousness. This vision of the Spirit of God not only confirmed Jesus' work on earth but reinforced what John had said when he told the crowds that 'I baptise you with water . . . but someone more powerful is going to come, and . . . he will baptise you with the Holy Spirit . . .' (see Matthew 3:11).

The final stage was the voice from heaven, which declared that '. . . This is my own dear Son, and I am pleased with him' (verse 17). The voice of God the Father brought the whole concept of the three characters of God together. At the River Jordan, the Father, Son and Holy Spirit acted as one to announce the beginning of reconciliation between the human race and God.

Distribute the pens and paper to the group and ask them to write down what they think the characteristics and behaviour are of a Father, a Son and what they think is the role of the Holy Spirit.

(Allow 5 minutes for this)

Put some of the group's ideas about God the Father, Son and Holy Spirit up on the wall for everyone to see. Suggest to the group that they should spend a few moments in quiet while they consider the concept of God as having three characters and as you read the following:

Lord,
    although I've no real idea
    how to understand the concept
    of you having three parts,
    I can relate to the idea
    that you know what it's like
    to have someone who
    acts as a parent,
    telling us what to do,
    when to do it,
    how to do it,
    and that it's for our own good
    (although we really don't want to do it,
    but who said anything about choice?),
    and you know something about being a parent,

wondering if their child
is going to be all right.
Are they doing as they have been told?
Who are they hanging around with?
And should they really be seen
with those less than desirable people,
who everybody says
are sure to be trouble with a capital 'T'?
And you know all about that Holy Spirit bit,
the part that most people,
would rather leave in the margins
of their memories,
where it's convenient to forget
and only drag out the details
on special occasions,
like weddings, funerals
and getting Easter eggs.
Isn't this Holy Spirit thing
supposed to be just as important?
You know, it's the bit
that Jesus said would be with us
all the time,
even when we feel useless,
powerless and everything-less?
Lord,
help me to appreciate
all that you are,
everything that you can be
to me,
and every person
on this large lump of earth.

TODAY'S SPECIAL

Something to bleat about!
John 1:29-42: The Lamb of God

Equipment:
postcards
stopwatch
flipchart
music and lyrics

Make sure that you have enough postcards for each member of the group. Before you get together write one of each of the following on the postcards:

Wild boar	Wart hog	Camel	Lamb	Slug
Orang-utan	Sloth	Hen	Earthworm	
Moth	Seagull	Pheasant	Crocodile	
Anteater	Termite	Tortoise	Cat	

Give each member of the group a postcard with one of the animal names written on it. The idea of the game is for one group member to start a story containing a reference to the animal named on their card. The group member has twenty seconds to tell the beginning of the story and then the person next to the first group member must carry on the story, remember to refer to the first animal mentioned and also include the animal named on their card. The next person must then refer to the previous two animals and include their named animal in the story. The story continues with each new person referring to the animals previously mentioned and including their own animal. Remember that each storyteller has only twenty seconds to tell their part of the story including references to all the other previously mentioned animals. The last group member must finish the story to include every named animal. The time allowed for each storyteller is important. The first few group members should have little difficulty mentioning the previous animals but the last few storytellers will find it increasingly hard to remember and include every animal.

(Allow 10 minutes for this activity)

Having something to say within a limited amount of time *and* trying to include everything that was said before is just a bit difficult!

Take a look at 'Lamb of God' (*The source*, 310) or 'All hail the Lamb' (*The source*, 6).

(Allow 5 minutes for this)

Ask the group what they thought of the lyrics to the song.

Read John 1:29-42.
In verse 29 of the reading, John shouts, '. . . here is the Lamb of God who takes away the sin of the world!' If someone were to shout that out today they'd get some very strange looks! But when everyone heard John describing Jesus as the 'Lamb of God' they understood exactly what he meant.

Our understanding of a lamb is something small, woolly and often found on a dining table covered in mint sauce (without the wool)! Unlikely as it may seem, a lamb had a very different meaning to the people of the New Testament.

One image of a lamb was as a symbol of strength, a conqueror. A second image was of the Passover Lamb (see Exodus 12). At the time John was speaking the Passover Feast wasn't far away. The story in Exodus is that the blood of a slain lamb was sprinkled on the doorposts of the Israelites' homes to protect them on the night they escaped from captivity in Egypt. The blood of the lamb protected the Israelites from destruction and enabled them to escape to safety. John made it very clear that Jesus was God's Lamb whose purpose was to become the sacrifice, which would take away the sin of the world.

At the same time as John spoke flocks of lambs would be shepherded towards Jerusalem to serve as the sacrifices for the Passover Feast. Just as Isaiah declared that there would be one who would be 'led like a lamb to the slaughter' (Isaiah 53:7) John also saw, in Jesus, the sacrificial lamb who would set the people free from the captivity of sin.

Ask the group to define the word 'Sacrifice'. Write some of their ideas onto the flipchart. Some of the ideas might include the words: offering, surrender, victim, or destruction. Are there different sorts of sacrifice? For example, going without something for a short time or giving something you own to someone else. Can the group suggest any different sorts of sacrifices that they can relate to in their own life?

(Allow 5 minutes for this task)

Place the flipchart with the 'sacrifice' definitions in the centre of the room. Ask the group to spend a few moments in quiet while you read the following:

Lord,
>if you ask me
>this *sacrifice* thing is a bit much.

What's the point?
How can giving something away
>mean so much?

Can you tell me
>how my actions
>can change the way other people
>behave, or think or believe?

I'm not so sure
>that the best thing to do
>isn't to keep everything I've got
>and to look after myself,
>just so that other people can see
>how good you are to me.

And, just think,
>you could give me even more good things,
>just to make the point, OK?

But there is one thing that niggles me.
Somewhere along the way,
>didn't you do something for me,
>that changed everything
>and made it possible to get to know
>God the Father, like a friend, a dad,
>someone you like to have around?

And, when I think about it a little more,
>didn't Jesus make all this a reality,
>by giving up everything he had,
>everything he could be,
>everything everybody wanted him to be,
>just so that me and you could get to know each other?

I'm not saying I understand this *sacrifice* thing,
>but however it works,
>it's made a difference to me,
>and I suppose that's the point of it all.

Lord, help me to make a difference
>to those people around me.

And, just a final thing,
>do you know anybody
>who might like
>half a packet of custard cream biscuits?

TODAY'S SPECIAL

Life to the full
Matthew 4:12-23: Jesus begins his work

Equipment:
A4 paper
pens
candle
matches
jam jar
music and lyrics

Give each group member a pen and a piece of paper. Ask the group to print their name vertically on the left-hand side of the paper. Pass the paper to the person on the immediate left of the writer. Ask that person to write a positive comment about the person whose name is on the paper. The comment must begin with the first letter in the person's name. Pass the paper to the left again and repeat the process using the second letter in the person's name. Continue until each piece of paper has been completed. After the exercise has finished, pass the sheet of positive comments to the 'named' person.

This exercise works best if the group has got to know each other during the past few weeks.

(Allow 10 minutes for this activity)

Reading comments about ourselves can be embarrassing but it can also be quite enlightening to learn just what people think of us.

Have a look at 'The happy song' (*The source*, 200) or 'Shine, Jesus, shine' (*The source*, 335).

(Allow 5 minutes for this)

The lyrics to the songs express something of the character of Jesus. Can the group identify words and phrases that express an emotion or a realisation of something special?

Read Matthew 4:12-23.

When John had been imprisoned Jesus moved to Capernaum which was in the territory of Zebulun and Naphtali. These regions were in northern Palestine whose population was predominantly gentile (non-Jewish).

For hundreds of years these regions had come under political and military attack and the people must have felt as if a dark cloud hung over the area. No one could feel totally safe and secure. Even if there weren't any physical acts of aggression, there was always plenty of political unrest that threatened the economic and social structure of the regions.

In the reading Matthew tells us of God's promise that although these people '. . . live in darkness, they will see a bright light . . .' (verse 16). This was a quote from the prophet Isaiah (Isaiah 9:1-2) who said that the darkness that hung over the land would be transformed into light. The Bible often uses the word 'light' to depict laughter and a life which is enjoyed fully. The word is particularly used to describe the presence of God. Matthew believed that Isaiah's prophecy was being fulfilled through the ministry of Jesus.

In verse 17 Jesus made it plain that only those people who understood that they had sinned against God and asked for his forgiveness had moved from darkness into the light. It was no coincidence that Jesus started his ministry in an area that had known so much trouble for so long. Jesus became the light in a dark area just as Isaiah had prophesied. Here was the opportunity to leave behind the feeling of insecurity and danger and accept the assurance of God's forgiveness and love. This was an offer to live life to the maximum, to take hold of the light and appreciate the presence of God.

Place a lit candle in the centre of the room. Leave the candle to burn for a few seconds and then place the jam jar over the candle and wait for the flame to go out. You can explain the simple scientific bit about the necessity of oxygen to maintain the flame if you wish.

Remove the jam jar and light the candle again. Explain to the group that just as the lack of oxygen stifles the flame so can things in our lives that cause us to ignore God. God wants us to live life to the full and only his light, or presence, will have an affect that will last an eternity.

(Allow 5 minutes for this)

As the candle burns ask the group to be quiet and concentrate on the flame. Read the following Psalm:

Psalm 36:7-10
Your love is a treasure,
    and everyone finds shelter in the shadow of your wings.
You give your guests a feast in your house,
    and you serve a tasty drink that flows like a river.
The life-giving fountain belongs to you,
    and your light gives light to each of us.
Our Lord, keep showing love to everyone who knows you,
    and use your power to save all whose thoughts please you.

TODAY'S SPECIAL

The when, where and why!

John 2:1-11: Jesus at a wedding in Cana

Equipment:
paper
pens
small stone or pebble for each group member
music and lyrics

Give each member of the group a piece of paper and a pen. Ask them to write the word 'When' in capital letters at the top of the page. Each person is to write a 'when' descriptor. For example: 'It was Christmas time and . . .' or 'Just as the alarm clock sounded . . .' or even 'It was a dark and stormy night . . .'. When they have completed this ask them to fold the piece of paper so that the 'when' descriptor is concealed and pass the paper on to the person immediately on their left. This person writes 'Where' on the paper in capital letters and suggests an idea for a place. For instance 'On the carpet . . .' or 'In the middle of the shopping centre' or even 'In the back of a pick-up truck . . .'. The same process is used as before with the paper folded to conceal the 'where' suggestion and the paper is passed on for a third time. The next person then writes the word 'Why' in capital letters and proceeds to write an explanation as to 'why'. Again, for example, 'Because she didn't like doughnuts' or 'Because the boy next door had a large bag of carrots for sale' or even 'Because the next-door neighbour's cat had just given birth to kittens'.

Pass the completed paper to the next person and then read the results!

(Allow 10 minutes for this activity)

Although for most things there is a 'when', 'where' and a 'why', we often forget to think about the relevance of these three 'Ws'.

Have a look at 'All my days' (*The source new songs*, 2) or 'Come, now is the time to worship' (*The source 2*, 662). Alternatively, you might like to look at the sketch on page 52.

(Allow 5 minutes for this)

What do the lyrics of the songs tell us about Jesus?

Read John 2:1-11.

The story of the wedding at Cana is a very popular episode in the life of Jesus. The first recorded miracle of Jesus gives us a sensational insight into the beginning of his ministry and the reaction of the people at the wedding feast. Unfortunately, the when, where and why are often over-looked.

Firstly, we know *when* the miracle happened. Jesus was at a wedding feast. He was obviously quite happy to be a guest at such an occasion and was certainly no boring, stiff-necked, killjoy who turned his nose up at a party. The wedding celebrations often went on for several days and were definitely not an occasion for a quick visit, say hello and throw an orange juice down your neck.

Jesus did not go around suggesting that celebrations and being happy were strictly no-go areas, it was quite the opposite. Throughout his ministry Jesus never turned down an opportunity to share in other people's happiness, give other people cause to celebrate or simply have a chat with a few friends over a quiet drink. Jesus wanted people to be happy and expected nothing less.

Secondly, John tells us exactly *where* the miracle happened. Jesus didn't go to some major event that attracted all the most influential movers in the land, or a celebration watched by huge crowds. The wedding at Cana took place in a small village, which most people would have difficulty locating on a map. The presence of Jesus brought God into the everyday lives of everyday people. It was the extraordinary taking place in the ordinary.

Thirdly, we can begin to understand *why* the miracle took place. It would have been a major embarrassment if the host ran out of wine before the celebrations were over. It was considered absolutely essential for the host to perform just as tradition expected. If anything happened that made it appear that the host was failing in his duty then everybody would know that the host was unable to provide the essential ingredients that made a wedding feast so important. Jesus performed the miracle so that an ordinary family would avoid the hurt and humiliation of failing in their duty.

At Cana Jesus acted out of understanding and sympathy for the people there. Jesus didn't make a big issue of the miracle, he simply understood what was needed and provided what was necessary. This was God getting involved in the everyday lives of everyday people to show just how much he cared, and he's still in the same business.

Give every member of the group a pebble or stone. Ask them to think of a situation in their own life in which they would like God to get involved. When they have done this ask them to place the pebble or stone on the floor in the centre of the room.

(Allow 5 minutes for this)

Once the group have each placed their pebble or stone on the floor ask them to remain quiet while you read the following prayer:

Lord,
    I can't always say exactly *when* I may need your help,
    or precisely *where* I'll need it,
    but I think I'll always know *why*
    I need your help,
    your love,
    your understanding,
    and the occasional bit of patience
    for those times when nothing I say or do seems right.
Why I need you around is simply because,
    no matter how hard I try not to
    screw everything up with such finesse,
    whatever I try to do
    always ends up with my own,
    totally unique,
    absolutely unmistakable,
    foot in mouth,
    finger in the eye,
    tread on foot trademark
    that everyone knows
    is my way of doing things,
    that nobody else would have thought of
    (or wouldn't even dream of doing if they had any sense).
What I'm saying, Lord,
    is that even when I do my best,
    it isn't always the best that everyone expects.
So, could we come to some sort of arrangement,
    where you get involved in my everyday life,
    every single day of my existence,
    to make sure
    that we all get used to having
    a touch of the extraordinary
    in our ordinary lives?

THE GRANNIES DISCUSS CONFETTI

Characters   Moll and Poll, the two Grannie gossip gangsters, are feeling a little perturbed. Even their radar-like ability for scandal, and other minor issues, hasn't prepared them for the latest news.

Scene   The Grannies are seated on a bench. They are dressed in mismatched clothes, old raincoats with brightly coloured aprons on the outside of their coats. Both have a carrier bag full of shopping which they occasionally shuffle around.

Props   Raincoat, dresses, headscarves, brightly coloured aprons and two carrier bags containing boxes of varying sizes. A bench-type seating arrangement.

Moll   *(Adjusts headscarf and peers into carrier bag. She rearranges a couple of items in the bag and then nods to Poll)* Nice day.

Poll   *(Sitting with her carrier bag on her lap)* Sort of.

Moll   *(Frowns)* Sort of?

Poll   *(Sniffs)* As I said.

Moll   Are you all right?

Poll   As well as can be expected . . .

Moll   *(Finishing Poll's sentence)* . . . Under the circumstances!

Poll   That's right.

Moll   *(Leans towards Poll)* And what circumstances might they be when they're at home?

Poll   *(Looks away from Moll)* Just circumstances that a sensitive woman, like myself, experiences from time to time.

Moll	*(Nudges Poll)* Really? *(Winks)*
Poll	*(Ignores Moll's wink)* Yes, really.
Moll	Do tell. I have very sensitive hearing for such sensitive people with sensitive subjects to discuss.
Poll	Who said anything about 'discussing' anything?
Moll	*(Nudges Poll again)* I did. Now, don't be so secretive and tell your old gossip pal what's on the agenda.
Poll	*(Looks from side to side)* Love!
Moll	*(Shocked expression)* Love?
Poll	That's what I said.
Moll	Are you sure?
Poll	As sure as I can be under the circumstances.
Moll	*(Nudges Poll . . . again)* You sly old fox.
Poll	*(Rubs arm where Moll nudged)* Nothing of the sort.
Moll	*(Claps hands together and then clasps her hands)* I never would have believed it.
Poll	It took me by surprise I can tell you.
Moll	And what does him indoors say about all of this?
Poll	It doesn't concern him.
Moll	*(Sits upright)* He doesn't suspect anything?
Poll	Why should he?
Moll	Well, you know. They say that you can always tell something's going on when people begin to change their habits.

Poll	He wouldn't notice anything. He's far too preoccupied with his aquarium.
Moll	*(Nods knowingly)* I understand. Mine can't keep his eyes off his geraniums. Sits talking to them all day. Strokes their leaves, brushes their petals and pampers them something rotten.
Poll	*(Nods in agreement)* Classic case of horticultural dementia.
Moll	*(Shrugs)* Still, at least you know where they are and that they're not up to something. *(Nudges Poll)* Talking about getting up to something, you were saying?
Poll	*(Rubs arm again)* I do wish you wouldn't keep nudging me. Mind you, I should have given him a nudge the last time I saw him.
Moll	*(Leans forward)* Him?
Poll	Yes, you know, young William.
Moll	Young William? He'll never see the bright side of sixty again. What on earth do you see in him?
Poll	See in him? Nothing, apart from someone who ignores the fact that we virtually grew up together, went to the same school, visit the same doctor and both have a niggling case of athlete's foot.
Moll	*(Pats Poll's knee)* They do say it's always good if you have a lot in common.
Poll	You would have thought so wouldn't you.
Moll	*(Frowns and then places a finger against her lips)* Just a moment. Didn't his son get married last week to that girl from the other side of town?
Poll	That's right. As I said, I should have nudged him to remind the old wrinkle to send me an invitation. It's no good waiting for that good-for-nothing husband of mine to go and remind young William to invite us.

Moll	*(Screws her face up)* This 'love' business. It wasn't anything to do with you and old slack-jaw then?
Poll	*(Looks shocked)* Well, I'll go to our dung heap and back. What gave you that idea?
Moll	*(Shakes her head)* Nothing, nothing at all.
Poll	All I was saying was that this love match between his son and the girl should have resulted in my receiving a wedding invitation.
Moll	From what I hear, it was a miracle that the wedding took place at all.
Poll	I heard that a miracle did take place.
Moll	The only miracle that I can see is that they both went through with the ceremony.
Poll	Well, our gossip sources differ. Let's just say that some sort of miracle took place.
Moll	If you say so. But I still think *(looks from side to side conspiratorially)* it was a miracle that he ever took up with her.
Poll	*(Nods)* Her parents are not from, what you might call, the right side of the street.
Moll	*(Nods in agreement)* Different side of the town. A little bit rougher than a coconut duvet.
Poll	Love's grand, though. It tends to ignore those little imperfections in a person's character.
Moll	Not so much 'little imperfections', more like a personality of a rubbish tip. Still, it were a miracle.
Poll	*(Nods)* Certainly was.
	(Both shuffle through their carrier bags)

TODAY'S SPECIAL

Emotional erosion
Matthew 6:25-34: Worry

Equipment:
balloons
flipchart
pen
wastepaper basket
music and lyrics

Give each group member a balloon. Ask each of them to inflate the balloon until it is approximately half-size; then stop the balloon from deflating by pinching the end of the balloon tight between fingers. Now, point to the first person on your left and ask them to name things that worry them. Draw a circle onto the flipchart and list the person's worries in the circle. Write that person's name below the circle. Ask the next person to name some of their worries and again draw a circle, write the worries in the centre and the person's name below the circle. Continue until every member of the group has contributed to the question.

Turn to the group and tell them to take a deep breath and blow up the balloon until they cannot blow any more. Repeat the exercise for every worry that they have named. This should cause a lot of giggles and result in some burst balloons!

(Allow 10 minutes for this)

Being worried about things can be a real headache, especially when we feel that no one else understands what we're going through.

Have a look at 'Your eye is on the sparrow' (*The source 2*, 1093) or 'Day by day' (*The Australian Worship Collection*, 9).

(Allow 5 minutes for this)

Ask the group if they felt that the lyrics helped them to appreciate how other Christians expressed their trust in God.

Read Matthew 6:25-34.
Explain to the group that the game with the balloons was one way to portray the way we behave as individuals. If you can imagine, we are all

similar to half-inflated balloons. We each have lots of everyday things that require our attention (what to wear, whether to stay at home or go out, whether to buy this or that) and we regularly deal with other things that happen less frequently (visits to the dentist, exams, tests, meeting new people). This is represented by the half-inflated balloon. All the extra worries continue to inflate the balloon until we either feel fit to burst or simply explode. Sometimes, even the normal everyday things seem to get too much and adding anything else to the list would appear to be the last straw.

Jesus explains that we should accept life as a gift from God and, as such, shouldn't worry about things that we have little or no control over. For instance, nobody knows what will happen to them from one day to the next. Disease and death are all around us and, although we should take care of our bodies, there is little point in worrying about every eventuality. Some people have become totally obsessive about their health and have gone to extremes to try and make sure that they don't expose themselves to any risk or infection. What a sad way to live a life!

Jesus points out that getting all worked up and anxious doesn't achieve a single thing; it's wasted energy and absolutely fruitless. He goes on to say that the flowers in the field don't spend all their energy worrying about the way they look and whether they'll still look beautiful tomorrow. The flowers are a part of God's creation and he has provided everything that they need.

Jesus tells us that it's pointless worrying about things that we can have no influence over. It's just as pointless spending all our time trying to make sure that we don't expose ourselves to any passing microscopic organism that just might give us a sniffle. Equally, it's a waste of energy worrying about everything that we see or read. We are encouraged to take each step with confidence, believing that God has taken care of us this far and will continue to do so. If you imagine a flight of stairs then each step represents a stage of God's provision which enables us to move forward confidently. If we take on every concern and worry which we become aware of then we are likely to explode! Build upon the small things and then take on the larger issues. Jesus isn't saying ignore the wider issues and become self-centred, quite the opposite, but we are totally ineffective if we are on the verge of exploding at any moment!

Ask each group member to hold a balloon and think about one issue which they consider to be giving them grief. Place the wastepaper basket in the centre of the room. After a few moments suggest that they take their balloon and place it in the wastepaper basket. Explain that placing the balloon in the basket represents the issue, which they have been considering, and how they've consigned it to the rubbish tip along with all the other issues, which cause us to feel as if we will explode!

After the group have placed their balloons in the basket, suggest that they spend a further few moments in quiet while you read the following prayer:

> Lord,
> I just can't take any more
> of these issues that are irritating,
> annoying, frustrating, aggravating,
> infuriating, bothering and any other 'ing' that you can think of.
> Sometimes, Lord,
> I feel as if nothing could make me feel
> down and out,
> trodden on and squashed
> out of all recognition,
> but then as soon as I open my mouth,
> or even think that everything
> might just be OK,
> something comes along
> out of nowhere,
> and suddenly
> everything
> is pear shaped.
> Is there some universal truth,
> that giving voice to your thoughts or feelings,
> even giving them brain room,
> somehow makes your head
> vulnerable to any passing
> mental brick or emotional boulder
> which is guaranteed to give you one major,
> all-time headache?
> Because if that's the case,
> I'm going into hibernation,
> for ever and ever amen!
> But, and it's only a small but,
> but if it's just the case
> that these things happen,
> whenever, however and forever,
> then I've got to admit,

that I haven't got a clue how to deal with them.
Right, just so that you and I know,
    from now on,
    I'm making it quite clear
    that I do not intend to try and sort anything,
    and all the other 'ings', on my own.
That's fair warning, Lord,
    that in future,
    in fact from this very moment,
    I'm putting every hassle that I know,
    and all those that are considering coming my way,
    into the rubbish basket,
    for you to help me deal with life
    and other assorted animals.

TODAY'S SPECIAL

Remarkable for this time of year!
Matthew 17:1-9: The true glory of Jesus

Equipment:
pen
two small pieces of card for every member of the group
music and lyrics
small cross
pebbles

Give every member of the group a pen and two pieces of card. Ask them to think of situations or phenomena which they may find confusing, baffling or just plain wacky! For instance: 'Why do you get the colour purple when you mix red and blue together?' or 'How do birds know which way to migrate?' or even 'Why does it hurt when I bang my head on a hard surface?' Ask each group member to write one question on their card to which they'd like an answer.

Collect all the 'question' cards and then ask the group to write an answer to their original question. It doesn't matter if they haven't got an actual answer for their original question, they can make up an answer which they think might be the real one!

Each answer should begin with the word 'because'. Again, collect all the cards once the group have finished.

Shuffle and distribute all the 'why' cards and then all the 'because' cards and ask each member to read their 'why' card followed by the 'because' card, creating such nonsense as: 'Why does eating loads of ice cream make you fat? Because of gravity!'

(Allow 10 minutes for this activity)

Many things intrigue us and often we struggle to find an explanation. Sometimes it may seem impossible to find an answer or even frightening that we cannot find a rational explanation for something.

Take a look at 'Say to those who are fearful' (*The American Worship Collection*, 79) or 'Our God is an awesome God' (*The American Worship Collection*, 71/*The source*, 418).

(Allow 5 minutes for this)

Ask the group how they think the lyrics to the song relate to the idea of strange events or frightening situations.

Read Matthew 17:1-9.
This episode in the life of Jesus is often referred to as the 'transfiguration'. At the start of the journey up the mountain, Peter, James and John must have thought that this was just another amble where Jesus could escape from the crowds, find a bit of peace and quiet and have a bit of a chat with the three disciples. But this was not your everyday mountain. For a start, it was a very high mountain and not something to be tackled on a hot day. You can imagine that Peter, feeling just a tad reluctant to keep pushing one foot in front of the other, begins to ask how much further and what is the point of all this, and either James or John pointing to the top of the mountain and saying 'up there!' You can almost hear Peter groan at the feeble joke and then gasp in astonishment as the appearance of Jesus suddenly changes beyond all recognition.

The jaw-dropping moment doesn't stop there. On top of this high and lonely mountain two other figures appear and begin talking with Jesus. Now, even for three disciples who've seen a sight or two over recent weeks, this is just a bit out of the ordinary. They must have wondered what was going on when a cloud started talking to them! Instantly, three blokes with previously tough reputations are transformed into dribbling wrecks. The second, slightly less impressive, transfiguration sees the three disciples extremely afraid. So afraid that they throw themselves onto the ground and shut their eyes, tight.

Almost immediately, Jesus tells the three wrecks to get up, open their eyes and not to be afraid.

Often we encounter situations or events that leave us frightened or confused and 'transfigured' into something that is almost unrecognisable from normal. It's a natural reaction to shut our eyes to whatever it is that's causing us to act human, and attempt to make the problem go away. We cannot expect to be know-it-all's or brave-as-a-brick types. There will always be situations that leave us dazed and confused where only the words of Jesus can lift us up and remind us that we are not on our own. Whatever is out of this world and totally remarkable to us is an everyday occurrence for Jesus, so don't be afraid.

Discuss with the group some of the things that cause us to be afraid or make us react in a way which is far from our normal behaviour. Do we all react in the same way to similar situations? How do we try to deal with situations that we feel are threatening?

(Allow 5 minutes for this task)

Place the cross in the centre of the room and give each member of the group one of the pebbles. Suggest to the group that the pebble represents their fears, questions or doubts. Ask them to place the pebble at the base of the cross as a symbolic action. By placing the pebble at the base of the cross they are putting their faith in Jesus to deal with the 'whatever' in their lives.

When they have each placed the pebble at the cross, read the following Psalm:

Psalm 25:1-2, 4-5
I offer you my heart, Lord God, and I trust you.
Don't make me ashamed or let enemies defeat me . . .
show me your paths and teach me to follow;
guide me by your truth and instruct me.
You keep me safe, and I always trust you.

TODAY'S SPECIAL   **The 'If' word**
Matthew 4:1-11: Jesus and the devil

Equipment:
fruit gums
flipchart and pen
music and lyrics

Divide the group into pairs. Nominate one person from each pair to be the 'talker'. Arrange each pair so that they are directly opposite each other. The 'non-talker' is then asked to 'stick' their tongue out while you place a fruit gum on the tip of the tongue. The tongue must remain 'out' while the 'talker' begins to describe all their favourite foods. Encourage the 'talker' to describe each food in full detail giving as much emphasis as possible to taste and aroma. The object of the game is to see how long the 'non-talker' can keep their tongue extended with the fruit gum intact!

As soon as the 'non-talker' succumbs to the inevitable and eats the fruit gum, the pair change roles and the game begins again.

The winners are whoever can talk their partner into submission the quickest and whoever can resist their partner's 'sweet' talk the longest.

(Allow 10 minutes for this activity)

Temptation is a word that we always associate with being negative. Have a look at 'When the cares of life come' (*The source new songs*, 78/ *The source 2*, 1055) or 'Seasons may change' (*The source new songs,* 56).

How did the lyrics deal with the question of temptation?

Read Matthew 4:1-11.
Before Jesus gets on with telling people about restoring their relationship with God, he goes on a walkabout in the desert. It's here that the devil decides to have a go at Jesus and put a bit of temptation his way.

Each time that the devil attempts to divert Jesus' attention away from God, it isn't so much the fact that the devil tries to get Jesus to eat bread, tempt him to demonstrate his authority or offer vast wealth, it's the little word 'if' that is used to sow the first seeds of doubt.

Most of the time we can feel confident about who we are, what we are doing or even where we are going, but it's when someone questions our motives with the 'if' word that the whole thing begins to unravel in our heads.

We can be fairly experienced or have a lot of ability but when the 'if' word is introduced it makes us question everything that we thought we knew or believed.

It's easy to feel confident about being a Christian when we are with a group of people who all think the same way, but when we are alone with a group of people who think a 'Christian' is a species of fish, then it's far from easy to feel quite so confident.

The 'if' word needs to be small so that it can squeeze into the briefest of sentences. It doesn't have to be said very loudly for it to have a huge impact. It's so small that it takes just a split second to write but it can take hours or even days for its effect to dissolve.

Before anyone labels the 'if' word as negative, it's important to say that it is, in fact, a very important word that we should all use. Jesus wasn't afraid to use the 'if' word or deal with the devil's use of it. The important thing is how we react to the 'if' word.

Each time that the devil used 'if', Jesus immediately referred to what God had to say on the subject. This wasn't merely reciting the Scriptures like a parrot but showing that he, Jesus, knew and understood what God was saying and what it meant for everyday living.

The same principle applies to us. We also need to be aware of what God has to say (read the Bible) and how it can affect the way we think and behave (pray and chat with God).

Being afraid of the question 'if' is often the result of being in a desert ourselves, a self-inflicted desert which is the result of choosing not to involve God in our day-to-day lives. So, rather than think negative, act positive, if you can!

Write the word 'temptation' along the left-hand side of the flipchart. Ask the group for examples of temptations that begin with the first letter of the word 'temptation', and so on. For instance: T: threats; E: envy; M: money; P: porn; T: taste; A: anger; T: teasing; I: ignorance; O: outburst; N: nagging.

Put all the definitions that the group think of onto the flipchart.

(Allow 5 minutes for this)

With the flipchart clearly visible to everyone, ask the group to be quiet while you read the following:

James 1:12-18
God will bless you, if you don't give up when your faith is being tested. He will reward you with a glorious life, just as he rewards everyone who loves him. Don't blame God when you are tempted! God cannot be tempted by evil, and he doesn't use evil to tempt others. We are tempted by our own desires that drag us off and trap us. Our desires makes us sin, and when sin is finished with us, it leaves us dead. Don't be fooled, friends. Every good and perfect gift comes down from the Father who created all the lights in the heavens. He is always the same and never makes dark shadows by changing. He wanted us to be his own special people, and so he sent the true message to give us new birth.

TODAY'S SPECIAL   **Born twice**

John 3:1-17: Jesus and Nicodemus

Equipment:
flipchart
paper and pens for each group member
music and lyrics

Display the following quiz on the flipchart:

1. gnikool

2. your hat
   keep it

3. keen surgeon

4. take

   take

5. ban   ana

6. options, options, options, options, options.

7.   man
   _____
   board

8. r/e/a/d/i/n/g/

9. X X

10. 21 October/21 October

Distribute the paper and pens and ask each member of the group to try and work out what each of the ten puzzles means.

The answers are:

1. Looking backwards

2. Keep it under your hat

3. Sharp operator

4. Double take

5. Banana split

6. Several options

7. Man overboard

8. Reading between the lines

9. Double cross

10. Double date

You might like to give the group this example before they attempt the puzzle:

GROUND
Feet
Feet
Feet
Feet
Feet
Feet
Answer = six feet underground!
(Allow 10 minutes for this activity)

Dealing with things we don't understand is difficult. It's always useful to ask someone for a clue!

Take a look at 'Almighty God, my redeemer' (*The Australian Worship Collection,* 1) or 'Salvation' (*The Australian Worship Collection,* 93).
(Allow 5 minutes for this)

Sometimes the lyrics to songs can be difficult to understand. Ask the group what they thought of the lyrics to the chosen song.

Read John 3:1-17.
When you fill in a form which asks you for your nationality, the majority of people will claim the nationality of the country where they were born, for example, English, Dutch, American, Australian or French. To many people this national identity is a form of pride, a sense of belonging.

In the Bible reading, Nicodemus is described as a Pharisee and a Jewish leader. To be a Pharisee was to be a member of an elite, a special group of people who thought of themselves as very different from the ordinary citizens. As a Jew, Nicodemus would have been extremely proud of his cultural heritage. Fearful of damaging his reputation he went at night to discuss some issues with Jesus. Jesus knew exactly who Nicodemus was and of his reputation. In response to a comment by Nicodemus, Jesus tells him that he must be born again!

Can you imagine the look on Nicodemus' face and the confusion that he must have felt? Because of a simple comment he was being told that his prestige and cultural heritage were meaningless! But, rather than argue and justify himself, Nicodemus asks how it is possible for a grown man to be born again.

To restore the relationship between God and humankind, Jesus came down from heaven to tell everyone of the good news about God's love. Later, when Jesus dies, we are told (Mark 15:38) that the curtain in the temple was torn from *top* to bottom. In other words God's love was brought down to earth to bring salvation (to be freed from the power of sin).

Before a person agrees that they've been living a life without God's love and living under the shadow of sin, they are outside the kingdom of God. To be a part of the kingdom of God, a person must acknowledge that they've ignored God's love and that Jesus died to become the bridge between humankind and God. At some stage Nicodemus must have asked God for his forgiveness and invited him to become the centre of his life. Nicodemus and everyone who asks for God's forgiveness turn their backs on their old life, in which they were vulnerable to the power of sin, and enter into a new life with God.

Through the Holy Spirit (which took the place of Jesus) we have a relationship with God which is precious. We are no longer subject to the power of sin, although we have a free will to get ourselves into all sorts of mess. As Christians we have placed our trust in God and refuse to ignore his love for each of us. Being born again is exchanging a way of life in which God has no part for one where we have an intimate relationship because of the sacrifice that Jesus made.

Using a new piece of flipchart paper, ask the group to name actions or types of behaviour which can interfere with our relationship with God. How can we deal with these actions and restore a healthy relationship with God?

(Allow 5 minutes for this)

Ask the group to be quiet for a few moments while you read the following:

1 John 1:1-6
. . . I am writing this so that you won't sin. But if you do sin, Jesus Christ always does the right thing, and he will speak to the Father for us. Christ is the sacrifice that takes away our sins and the sins of the world's people. When we obey God, we are sure that we know him. But if we claim to know him and don't obey him, we are lying and the truth isn't in our hearts. We truly love God only when we obey him as we should, and then we know that we belong to him. If we say we are his, we must follow the example of Christ.

TODAY'S SPECIAL   **It goes deep**
John 4:5-42: Jesus and the Samaritan woman

Equipment:
pen and paper for each member of the group
flipchart
wastepaper basket
music and lyrics

Give each member of the group a piece of paper and a pen. Ask them to think about all the things that they find difficult to tolerate in other people. For instance, cultural behaviour, accents or eating habits.
Suggest to the group that they choose one particular thing which they find most annoying and write it on their piece of paper. Chat about some of the 'annoyances' and write some of them onto the flipchart. The group should keep their piece of paper for later.
(Allow 10 minutes for this activity)

Cultural behaviour is only 'visible' to other people. We are rarely aware that some of our behaviour may be seen as 'culturally annoying' to others.

Have a look at 'As sure as gold is precious' (*The source 2*, 636) or 'Come, now is the time to worship' (*The source 2*, 662).
(Allow 5 minutes for this)

Ask the group whether they thought the words of the songs spoke about being 'different'.

Read John 4:5-42.
The Pharisees had been active in spreading some malicious gossip suggesting that Jesus and John the Baptist were competing with each other to see who could baptise the most people. Although this wasn't true, and even John had acknowledged that he wasn't good enough to tie Jesus' shoelaces, the gossip had annoyed a lot of people who were wondering whether any of the rumours were true.

Rather than ignore the situation, Jesus decided to leave the area and make his way back to Galilee.

At this time, the map of Palestine would have shown Judea at the bottom, Galilee at the top and Samaria sandwiched in between. Looking at the map, the most obvious route for Jesus to take would have been to take the direct road from Judea to Galilee. However, to the majority of Jews this would not have been an acceptable route. Instead they would have travelled east, then north and then west to avoid going anywhere near Samaria.

The relationship between the communities of Samaria and Judea were cool, verging on hostile. No self-respecting Jew would ever be seen near a Samaritan or walk anywhere near Samaria.

Several hundred years before, the area of Samaria had been invaded by the Assyrians who had taken the Jews, who lived in that area, captive. After a while the Jews and Assyrians had intermarried and, when they returned to Samaria, they became known as the Samaritans.

The Jews of Judea themselves had been taken captive by the Babylonians, but the Jews had refused to intermarry and, when they returned home claimed to have retained their pure Jewish blood. From that time, the Jews and the Samaritans had developed a level of hostility rarely seen away from a battlefield.

Jesus chose to ignore the cultural differences and instantly displayed an important aspect of God's love; that his love was for everyone irrespective of race, colour or culture.

Even after leaving the malicious gossip behind, Jesus still chose to be controversial and do the very thing that was unheard of for a Jew to do. Jesus didn't take the shorter route because he couldn't face walking any further than he had to, nor did he take the shorter route because he wanted to get home as quickly as possible. He took the direct route through the heart of Samaria to express God's heart for everyone.

Jesus still takes the direct route, direct to each one of us irrespective of who or what we are. God doesn't let culture, race, colour or tradition alter the fact that he loves each of us passionately. Perhaps we should also apply a little bit of God's perspective to our relationships?

Look at those annoying things that the group identified earlier (refer to the flipchart).

- What can we do to avoid getting annoyed?
- Should we try to be more understanding of other types of behaviour?
- Is it possible that other people may find our behaviour annoying?

- Why are we sometimes intolerant of other people?

Ask the group to take the piece of paper on which they've written their 'annoyances' and, without looking at it again, screw the paper into a ball. Keep hold of the 'ball' for a moment.
(Allow 5 minutes for this task)

Place a wastepaper basket in the centre of the room. Ask the group to place their paper 'ball' into the basket. Once this has been done, pray the following prayer:

Lord,
    I suppose I don't like to think about it too much,
    you know,
    all those annoying ways that *other* people
    behave, act, speak and just, well, you know, live.
Why can't they all be like me?
It would make things so simple.
Just imagine,
    no hassles over language,
    no arguments over how or what to eat,
    no disputes over borders or land,
    no complicated debates about nationality,
    no violent confrontations about race,
    or ethnic origins.
No pointing fingers
    about the way people look, their skin tone –
    in fact, no problems whatsoever.
But, there again,
    I suppose,
    knowing the human race to be what it is,
    sooner or later
    we'd find something to argue about,
    and someone, somewhere,
    would claim to be superior to other people,
    even though
    we all bleed when we're cut,
    we all cry when we're sad,
    we all crumble to dust,
    when death stakes its claim.
Lord,
    I'm just so thankful

that, despite who we are
or what we may claim to be,
you love us unconditionally,
with no cultural filters
to weed out the undesirable elements
who you'd rather not have anything to do with.
Your love knows no boundaries,
nor skin tones,
or anything else for that matter.
You love us, full stop, period, without end,
for ever and ever.
Amen to that!

TODAY'S SPECIAL   **Healing light**

John 9:1-41: Jesus heals a man born blind

Equipment:
flipchart and pen
paper and pen for each group member
candle
music and lyrics

Write, in large letters, the word 'SIN' on the flipchart. Ask the group to discuss the idea of sin using some of the following questions:

- What is sin?
- Identify different actions or types of behaviour which are considered sinful.
- Are some forms of sin more or less acceptable than others?
- Is a type of behaviour considered acceptable by one person but as sinful by another?
- Do we have to deal with sin?

Write some of the group's responses onto the flipchart.

(Allow 10 minutes for this activity)

Talking about the nature of sin can seem quite negative, but the reality is that we live in a world where sin, or wrongdoing, creeps into our everyday existence.

Have a look at 'Can a nation be changed?' (*The source*, 62) or 'I'm accepted, I'm forgiven' (*The source*, 217).

(Allow 5 minutes for this)

Do the lyrics provide any clues as to how we can deal with sin?

Read John 9:1-41.

When we are faced with situations or have behaved in a way which we are not too impressed with ourselves, there is a tendency to see if we can shift the blame or responsibility onto someone or something else.

Often we question why something happens and wonder if there is a God. If he exists why do accidents happen or why do people act so violently towards each other? Do some people deserve what happens to them? These are not new questions. Even the disciples questioned what was going on and whether disease or illness was a result of someone's wrongdoing.

In verse 2 of the reading, the disciples ask Jesus whether it was his parents' sin or the man's sin that led to him being born blind. Jesus answers with an emphatic 'No!'

It is easy to blame God for something which we consider unfair or unjust. We can meet someone or see a situation which makes us feel angry at the injustice of it. The question 'why' echoes around our heads until we can no longer pretend to be satisfied with being told that we should be thankful that we're not like 'that'.

Jesus made it extremely clear that we live in a world which is corrupt and where evil will always attempt to destroy what is good. The very purpose of God sending Jesus to eventually act as our sacrifice was because sin had invaded every aspect of life. But, because Jesus had power over sin and death he could turn a desperate situation into one of rejoicing.

The presence of Jesus and his actions became a light in a world which was choked by the shadow of sin. Even today, through the Holy Spirit, Jesus acts as a light in situations where it seems impossible to see any light.

We may never know the answers to some of the world's problems but the promise of Jesus to be a light in the darkness is a constant reassurance when the shadows begin to blot out the sun.

Give each member of the group a piece of paper and a pen. Ask them to think of a situation, or someone, they feel needs the light of Jesus. The issue can be global, national, local or personal. It doesn't matter if it's only important to the group member or if it concerns a lot of people. Ask the group to write the issue onto the piece of paper and attach it to a notice board so that it acts as a reminder for everyone to chat to God about that particular issue.

Place the candle in the centre of the room and light it for everyone to see. Suggest to the group that they are quiet and think about the issue which they have posted onto the notice board. Read the following:

Psalm 142:1-5
I pray to you, Lord. I beg for mercy.
I tell you all my troubles,
    and whenever I feel low, you are there to guide me.
A trap has been hidden along my pathway.
Even if you look, you won't see anyone
    who cares enough to walk beside me.
There is no place to hide, and no one really cares.
I pray to you, Lord!
You are my place of safety,
    and you are my choice in the land of the living.
Please answer my prayer. I am completely helpless.

TODAY'S SPECIAL   **Sleeping it off**
John 11:1-45: The death of Lazarus

Equipment:
glass bowl (shallow)
table-tennis ball
flour
music and lyrics

Ask the group to divide themselves into pairs. Place the shallow glass bowl on the floor and put the table-tennis ball into the bowl. The first pair kneel opposite each other with the bowl between them. The object of the game is to see who can blow the ball out of the bowl first.

Continue with the other pairs and then have the winners from each pair compete against each other. Finally, have two unbeaten players ready to compete to find out who's the ultimate champion. However, just to make things a little more interesting, both players are to be blindfolded. Just before the players are ready to 'blow', tip a cup of flour into the bowl and let the game begin!

(Allow 10 minutes for this activity)

Ask the two finalists how they felt when the unexpected happened (once they have forgiven you!).

Take a look at 'Well, I was in need' (*The Australian Worship Collection*, 114) or 'You love me as you found me' (*The Australian Worship Collection*, 131). Alternatively, you might like to look at the sketch on page 79.

(Allow 5 minutes for this)

Sometimes we can sing songs but the words don't really sink in or mean anything to us. Do any of the group agree with this statement?

Read John 11:1-45.
Lazarus was a really good friend of Jesus. So when Jesus received word that Lazarus was sick you would have thought that the natural reaction would be to get up straightaway and go and see how he was. John tells

us that Jesus loved Martha, Mary and their brother Lazarus but instead of rushing to them he stayed where he was for another two days.

The disciples may have thought that Jesus was being cautious and didn't want to go Judea because he had been threatened with being stoned to death. When Jesus announced that he was now ready to visit Lazarus the disciples were totally surprised and just a little bit concerned for their own safety as well!

When Jesus said that Lazarus was simply asleep the disciples must have thought, 'Great! That means he's getting better and so we don't have to walk into danger.' But then Jesus made it quite plain that he meant Lazarus was actually dead!

Before, and during, the time of Jesus, death was feared by everyone. Death didn't seem to respect anyone and there seemed no way of defeating the finality of it. However, to Jesus, death wasn't to be feared and was subject to his power and authority. Although the disciples were probably not aware of the relevance of the situation, Jesus was making a vital statement concerning his own death and resurrection. Death couldn't hold him and it didn't have any power over him.

When Jesus finally reached Lazarus' home, he spoke to him as if he'd simply been asleep. Jesus didn't speak with sadness in his voice and certainly didn't speak with a questioning voice. It wasn't 'Lazarus, come out . . . if you can', or 'Lazarus, can you hear me?' Jesus spoke with authority because he knew that nothing was more powerful than God. Even before he told Lazarus to come out, Jesus thanked God for answering his prayers! This wasn't because Jesus was unsure what God wanted to do or that he needed to boost his confidence, it was purely because Jesus wanted to encourage those around him to have faith in a God who expressed his love even in the face of death.

If God can express his love in this way, surely we can begin to depend on him for the slightly less difficult situations which we face each day.

Ask the group if they have any direct experience of putting their trust in God for something or whether they have heard of other people's experiences. Have theses experiences made any difference to the individual's 'faith'?

Is it possible to always have faith in God, for everything? Or, if we are honest with ourselves and each other, does our level of trust in God depend on how we feel and what's going on in our lives at the moment?

(Allow 5 minutes for this)

Ask the group to be quiet while you read the following prayer:

Lord,
    I've heard that
    Jesus said if you had faith
    the size of a mustard seed
    then you could do amazing things.
Well, Lord,
    I'm not sure
    how big a mustard seed is exactly,
    but I think that my sort of faith
    doesn't compare with that of the seed.
My faith is, well, sort of,
    precisely, or thereabouts,
    about as big
    as a speck of dust
    or even smaller.
It might be better
    to look at my faith through a microscope,
    and then, just possibly,
    you might see a tiny,
    or even smaller,
    speck in the distance.
I'm not quite proud of this fact, Lord,
    I'm even a bit embarrassed really.
But at least I'm not going to shout my mouth off
    about something I know very little about.
So, I think we've got a bit of work to do,
    you know, me and you, Lord,
    because there's not a lot I can do,
    to change the situation,
    but I've heard that you can do
    sort of amazing things,
    out of nothing, nowhere,
    in the blink of an eye, sort of.
And I was wondering,
    if we can get together on this one,
    and maybe, just maybe,
    I might be able to see a difference
    in the way I trust you.
And that really would be a miracle.

THE GRANNIES SENSE A TOUCH OF MORTALITY

Characters	The two Grannies, Moll and Poll, are rather subdued. Recent news has given them a feeling of mortality, which they'd prefer not to experience.
Scene	They're both dressed in sombre clothing and sitting at a small table sipping tea. A newspaper lies open on the table.
Props	Sombre (dark) clothing with headscarves. Table and two chairs. Teapot and two cups. Large format newspaper.

Poll (*Takes a sip of her tea and then groans*) Ooooh!

Moll Is there something wrong with the tea? (*Strokes the side of the teapot*) It's a fresh brew, best tea leaves and I used the water from my hot water bottle too!

Poll (*Grimaces*) I wondered what the aftertaste was.

Moll (*Purses lips*) Manners, Poll, manners!

Poll Tell that to my feet.

Moll Feet? What have they got to do with anything?

Poll They've been giving me some stick recently.

Moll Well, what can you expect. They've seen some miles, they have.

Poll (*Leans forward and massages a foot*) I was hoping they'd see me through a few more winters, too.

Moll Don't see why they shouldn't. Look after them and they'll look after you.

Poll I'm not sure they're returning the compliment, though.

Moll (*Sips her tea*) Anyway, your feet are the least of your troubles.

Poll	*(Pauses, sipping her tea. Holds cup slightly away from mouth)* What troubles?
Moll	*(Taps newspaper)* Read the obituaries recently?
Poll	*(Pulls a face)* Not quite compulsive reading.
Moll	The obituaries seem to contain more news about some of our old friends than the rest of the paper.
Poll	Do I sense a touch of mortality creeping in?
Moll	A touch? It's more like someone driving a herd of cows through my life.
Poll	*(Smiles)* And leaving a load of aromatic debris behind?
Moll	*(Sniffs)* Please, don't be so common.
Poll	Since when did being 'common' cause you a problem?
Moll	As long as you don't say 'common as muck' that's all.
Poll	*(Raises eyebrows)* Would I?
Moll	*(Taps newspaper again)* Martha Tilbury got her name in the obituaries last week.
Poll	Martha? Why, she's younger than the both of us!
Moll	Precisely.
Poll	*(Takes a sip of tea)* It certainly makes you think.
Moll	Well, don't think about it for too long or you'll still be in mid-thought when your name appears in the same place as Martha's.
Poll	*(Shudders)* Ooh, the very thought.
Moll	Sssh. Leave the thinking for those who've got time on their hands.

Poll	Like Martha?
Moll	Surely there's not much life in her thinking-tackle now?
Poll	Are you implying that death is a sort of breathtaking, final event which is the last day of the rest of your life?
Moll	Well, it's certainly nature's way of telling you to take things easy from now on.
Poll	It certainly would cut the cost of your telephone bills.
Moll	And every other bill for that matter.
Poll	*(Pauses to sip her tea and stare into space)*
Moll	Hey! What are you thinking?
Poll	That when I was young, death was just a distant rumour.
Moll	*(Nods)* And now you realise that it's not a rumour but a certainty?
Poll	The only thing in life you can bank on.
Moll	*(Shrugs)* I don't see how a bank has anything to do with it. My Mum always used to say that it's no good leaving money behind, someone will only go and spend it. Much better to leave nothing behind and leave them all guessing what you did with your money.
Poll	*(Shudders)* Yuck, all this talk of death and our limited mortality makes me feel all cold.
Moll	Your temperature will surely depend on whether you're going *(looks up)* up or *(looks down)* down!
Poll	I don't like to think about it.
Moll	*(Sips tea)* As long as I get a nice cup of tea in the morning, to get me started, I don't mind.

Poll	I think death's a little bit more than a blend of tea.
Moll	Never underestimate a refreshing cup of tea.
Poll	It'd take a damn good tea blend to refresh you after you've got your name in the obituaries.
Moll	Steady! Thou shalt not take the name of thy tea blend in vain.
Poll	No offence meant, I'm sure.
Moll	None taken.
Poll	*(Holds teacup in both hands near mouth)* It still makes you think.
Moll	Quit with the thinking.
Poll	*(Nods towards the newspaper)* Can't help it with the obituary page staring me in the face.
Moll	*(Folds newspaper)* Gone but not forgotten.
Poll	I hope that's what they say about me when I make the ultimate shopping trip.
Moll	That's a nice way of looking at it. *(Sits back and looks up)* Death, one continuous shopping experience. Browsing through the shelves of various purchases we've made in our lives, checking for the bargains, wincing at the over-priced stuff and tut-tutting at the list of additives which added nothing to your life whatsoever.
Poll	I wonder whether God's ever thought of a buy one get one free sort of offer.
Moll	Make a lot of economic sense, that would. Why waste all that hard-earned experience on a youngster. Much better to come to the end of one episode, take a quick sleep, wake up, have a cup of tea and take up where you left off.
Poll	You could have a sort of reward card that you collect points on. Then you can trade them in for special little items like meeting a tall, dark handsome man with all his own teeth.

Moll	*(Jerks her head to indicate something behind her)* Obviously didn't have enough points on my card when I came to choose him, did I!
Poll	*(Takes a sip of tea)* Bargains are difficult to find.
Moll	I'm not sure I got a bargain, more of a sale of old stock!
Poll	*(Shrugs)* I think mine was from a closing-down sale.
Moll	Isn't that what death is, a closing-down sale?
Poll	I'm not so sure about the sale bit, but closing down seems most appropriate.
Moll	*(Takes a sip of her tea and sighs)* I sometimes think that certain parts of my body are closing down prematurely.
Poll	*(Sits back)* You're not going to go into specifics, are you?
Moll	*(Ignores Poll)* I remember. It was ten years back *(nudges Poll)* you recall, it was when I had that spot of bother with my plumbing.
Poll	*(Frowns and then raises eyebrows)* Ah, yes, I do remember. You tried all sorts of pills and potions before you plucked up the courage to see Old Doc Rippum.
Moll	Nothing to do with courage. *(Sniffs)* It was more to do with eliminating all possible alternatives before I troubled the good doctor.
Poll	If my memory serves me correctly, you didn't use the word 'good' doctor after you went to see him. It was something like . . .
Moll	*(Interrupts quickly)* . . . nothing of the sort. I was a trifle upset. At my age, having someone suggest that your plumbing problems are nothing more than a simple case of a worn washer, well *(sits haughtily in chair)* I ask you, the impertinence of the man.
Poll	And did the, er, 'condition' go away?

Moll	*(Places cup on table, straightens her apron and pats her headscarf)* Not exactly, I simply drink in moderation now.
Poll	*(Places hands to each side of face in mock surprise)* 'Moderation'! I've never known you to drink, or do anything for that matter, in moderation.
Moll	*(Annoyed)* Excuse me!
Poll	That's what you always say just before you fall flat on your face after a tipple.
Moll	*(Takes a sip of tea and places cup in saucer, making the cup rattle)* How could you imply such a thing?
Poll	Quite easy. I simply state the facts. Anyway, it's a wonder your 'drinking in moderation' hasn't led you to a place in the obituaries.
Moll	A little wine for the stomach's sake.
Poll	A 'little' wine? I think something more like the deluge that Noah experienced would be a more apt analogy.
Moll	You can't talk.
Poll	At least there's nothing wrong with my 'washer'.
Moll	That may be all that's in working order.
Poll	*(Smiles and leans across to pat Moll's hand)* That may be so, but we've still got plenty of life left in the old bones.
Poll	You'd better believe it! Let's drink to life, love and gossip.
Moll	*(Lifts cup and holds it towards Poll)* Live to gossip.
Poll	Love to gossip.
Moll	Here's to the future.
Poll	*(Lifts cup in the same manner)* Cheers.

TODAY'S SPECIAL   **Not what was expected!**
Matthew 21:1-11: Jesus enters Jerusalem

Equipment:
pen and paper for each group member
music and lyrics

Give everyone a pen and piece of paper. Tell them that they have just been given £1,000 to spend. Ask them to write what would be on their spending spree list.

After they've done this, apologise and say that the money was not for them but to be spent on people who they consider to be in need of financial help (they are not to consider themselves in this!).

Once they've completed the second task, ask them how they felt when they were told that the money wasn't actually for them.

(Allow 10 minutes for this activity)

Our expectations are sometimes altered in ways that we'd rather not experience.

Take a look at 'Love songs from heaven' (*The source 2*, 884/*The source new songs*, 41) or 'O sacred King' (*The source new songs*, 50).

(Allow 5 minutes for this)

Sometimes what we expect and the reality are not quite the same. Ask the group what their expectations are, based upon the lyrics of the chosen song.

Read Matthew 21:1-11.
In Jerusalem expectations were running high. For the priests and religious leaders it was a time of celebrating the Passover and, possibly, they might at last get their hands on the one person who was a real pain to them: Jesus.

For the ordinary people the Passover was also a time of celebration but their expectations were even higher than normal. They had seen and heard all of the things that Jesus had done recently and they'd heard of his being referred to as the 'Son of David' (see Matthew 20:31). The term 'Son of David' was a title which the Jewish people understood to mean the messianic king, a new ruler who would liberate his people from foreign rule. Even the Mount of Olives was significant as the prophet Zechariah had spoken of the Messiah making a stand there against all of God's enemies (see Zechariah 14:4).

All the evidence pointed to something exceptional, something of the utmost importance. The crowds gathered and welcomed Jesus as he entered Jerusalem on a donkey (a king would ride a donkey as someone who came in peace). Yet within a week this Messiah, the 'Son of David' was dead.

The priests and religious leaders were content. Order had been restored and this nuisance, Jesus, had been dealt with. The Jewish people's hopes had been dashed against the wood of the cross. Expectations seemed to count for nothing where death was concerned.

Just as Jesus had shown time and again, death had no power over him. His mission was to act as the ultimate sacrifice, once and for all, so that the relationship could be finally restored between God and the people. It was obvious that the majority of people hadn't really understood what Jesus had been saying. The freedom he offered and the authority that he'd shown were not to deal simply with Roman rule but to end the rule of evil.

Sometimes our expectations are limited to what we can see immediately in front of us. Perhaps we should try to see things from God's perspective?

Ask the group to discuss what their expectations are for the future. For example: qualifications, jobs, marriage, health and possessions. Try and encourage the group to consider their expectations from God's point of view. Look at what the Bible might have to say about each of their ideas.

(Allow 5 minutes for this task)

Ask the group to spend a few moments reflecting on their ideas for the future while you read the following:

Psalm 139:1-3, 23-24
You have looked deep into my heart, Lord,
    and you know all about me.
You know when I am resting or when I am working,
    and from heaven you discover my thoughts.
You notice everything I do and everywhere I go . . .
    look deep into my heart, God, and find out everything I am thinking.
Don't let me follow evil ways,
    but lead me in the way that time has proved true.

TODAY'S SPECIAL   **You'd better believe it!**

Matthew 28:1-10: Jesus is alive

Equipment:
pen and paper for each group member
music and lyrics

Give each member of the group a pen and a piece of paper. Read out each of the following statements and ask them to write whether they think the statement is true or false.

1. St John was the only one of the 12 apostles to die a natural death.
2. A monkey was awarded a medal and promoted to the rank of corporal during World War 1.
3. Sliced bread was patented by a Mrs P. Ride in 1954.
4. An old custom, when drinking, was to throw a pinch of salt over your left shoulder to keep the devil away.
5. The cost of the first pay-toilets in England was one penny.
6. In 1647 the English Parliament abolished Christmas.
7. The word 'Abracadabra', used by stage magicians, was originally intended to cure hay fever.
8. In Victorian times there was a law which prohibited the wearing of a flat cap on a boat.
9. Gabriel and Michael are the only two angels to be named in the Bible.
10. The national flag of Austria was designed by an Irishman.

The answers are: 1. True; 2. True; 3. True; 4. False; 5. True; 6. True ; 7. True; 8. False; 9. True; 10. False.

Total the scores and see who was able to make any sense (or good guesswork) of the strange statements.

(Allow 10 minutes for this activity)

There are many things which appear to be beyond belief, but just because they are slightly strange doesn't mean that there isn't something totally amazing about them.

Have a look at 'I know he rescued my soul' (*The source 2*, 768/*The Australian Worship Collection 2*, 34) or 'Lifted up in our hopelessness' (*The Australian Worship Collection 2*, 62).

(Allow 5 minutes for this)

Did the group consider any of the lyrics to the chosen song to be difficult to believe?

Read Matthew 28:1-10.

The resurrection of Jesus was a major disappointment for all the religious leaders and politicians who thought that they'd got rid of a huge problem. Almost immediately, rumours were spread in an attempt to discredit the eyewitness accounts of those who had seen Jesus buried and those who'd seen him alive again.

The rumours were an attempt to suggest that the people who claimed that Jesus was alive were at best mistaken and at worst desperate frauds.

It was both Mary Magdalene and the other Mary who'd watched Jesus placed into the tomb and the large rock rolled across the entrance. The same two women were the first to discover that the rock had been rolled away and the tomb empty.

Rumours that the tomb had been robbed of Jesus' body were put around despite the tomb being guarded by Roman soldiers who knew they would suffer a severe punishment if they were to fall asleep or desert their duty. More importantly, would anyone have believed that these soldiers would do nothing while the disciples took the body of Jesus away (see verse 13)?

Another rumour, which claimed Jesus had merely fainted and then recovered in the cold tomb, ignores the fact that it would take an extremely strong person to roll the rock away from the tomb entrance. This also ignores the fact that Jesus had suffered a beating, whipping, dragged a heavy section of wood around the streets, been nailed to a cross and then had his side punctured by a spear.

The one overriding fact remains that Jesus rose again exactly as he had said he would. Despite the evidence there were plenty of people, and still are, who refused to believe that although it is an absolutely weird thing to happen, Jesus did rise from the dead and appear to hundreds of people.

Although strange to believe, Jesus suffered, died and rose again to fulfil everything that God intended. The facts, hard to believe or appreciate at times, remain that God loves us and went to extreme lengths to make it possible for us to get personal with the Creator.

Read the account of the resurrection again. Ask the group to imagine that they are a group of detectives who are the first to arrive on the scene after the reports of Mary Magdalene and Mary. How would they assess the evidence? What questions would they have asked? What conclusion would they have come to?

(Allow 5 minutes for this task)

Suggest to the group that they think about how the disciples would have felt when they heard, and later saw the evidence, of Jesus' resurrection.

While the group consider this, read the following:

Psalm 145:1-3, 5-9
I will praise you, my God and my King,
    and always honour your name.
I will praise you each day and always honour your name.
You are wonderful, Lord, and you deserve all praise,
    because you are much greater than anyone can understand . . .
I will keep thinking about your marvellous glory
    and your mighty miracles.
Everyone will talk about your fearsome deeds,
    and I will tell all nations how great you are.
They will celebrate and sing about your matchless mercy
    and your power to save.
You are merciful, Lord!
You are kind and patient and always loving.
You are good to everyone,
    and you take care of all your creation.

TODAY'S SPECIAL   **Sent to talk**
John 20:19-31: Jesus appears to his disciples

Equipment:
flipchart
pen
music and lyrics

Ask for a volunteer. Explain to them that they are going to draw an object onto the flipchart. Have prepared a series of pictures which are unusual, odd or totally wacky. Now, ask for another person to describe one object for the first volunteer. The two volunteers must not face each other or look around. The second volunteer must describe the drawing using simple terms. For example: draw a vertical line twenty centimetres high, or draw a circle about the size of a tennis ball. The second volunteer must not use any words which give any clues about the object. When both volunteers think they have finished view the finished product.

Ask for another volunteer and show them a picture. Select another person who is to draw the object onto the flipchart. Select two more people to draw another picture, only allow these two people to face each other and the drawer may ask questions to check that they are doing the right thing. The person explaining the drawing must still not use any descriptive words which explain the whole picture.

Each of the drawings will be a variation on the original but the second picture should be closer to the actual picture than the previous drawing.

(Allow 10 minutes for this activity)

Sometimes our attempts to explain things fall short of our hopes. Why not have a look at 'Who sees it all' (*The source*, 580) or 'What kind of love is this' (*The source*, 568).

(Allow 5 minutes for this)

Do the words of the lyrics explain things clearly?

Read John 20:9-31.
As Jesus appeared to the disciples, he greeted them in a traditional Jewish way: 'Peace to you.' Peace was not quite what the disciples felt at

that moment in time. They'd locked themselves in the room for fear of the Jewish leaders.

After greeting them again, just in case they'd not understood the first time, Jesus then tells them that he's going to send them OUT! Just what the disciples wanted to hear!

Firstly, Jesus told the disciples that he was sending them, just as the Father had sent him to preach the good news to everyone.

Secondly, Jesus wasn't sending them out to face the world alone, he gave them the Holy Spirit who would enable them to carry on where Jesus had left off.

Finally, he gave them the authority, and power, to forgive anyone's sins. This wasn't a simple throwaway line that was said as an afterthought. Jesus gave the disciples the ability to forgive sins because he, Jesus, had become the ultimate sacrifice and paid the price of sin for all time.

As a result of the disciples being sent out, and communicating the good news of Jesus, we too have the opportunity of accepting Jesus as God's son, who has made it eternally possible for us to be free from the effects of sin, and become part of the family of God.

Discuss what the group feel is difficult or even embarrassing about telling other people about Jesus. Why do we find it difficult? Does everyone feel this way, why? Is it a lack of confidence or a lack of faith that makes it difficult to share what we know about Jesus?

(Allow 5 minutes for this task)

Encourage the group not to feel negative or dejected if they find it hard to talk about Jesus to other people. Explain that what they may feel doesn't alter the fact that God loves them. It doesn't matter what they do and don't do, God's love remains the same.

Ask the group to be quiet for a few moments while you read the following prayer:

Lord,
    you know that I find it difficult
    to talk
    to you without wondering
    whether I'm talking to myself,
    or that you're possibly too busy

listening to loads of other people,
who've got lots of things to ask you about,
like suffering, loss, pain, hurt, doubts,
anger, injustice, frustration,
and all the other things that make life too
complicated
for humans to deal with anything
successfully.
So I suppose that what I'm trying to say
is that it might seem
trivial or daft
to chat to you about
everyday things that make me
laugh, smile, frown or sulk.
I'm not so sure that you want to hear
about all the little bits and pieces
that are my life.
But, just thinking about it,
if all you had to listen to were
groans, moans, grumps, complaints,
questions and pleas,
then you might like
to hear some of the funnier bits of life,
just to give you something to smile about,
or laugh or cry.
So, if you don't mind,
I'll waffle on about this and that,
and add the occasional moan,
and you can, if you want to,
tell me what you think,
or what makes you laugh,
or cry,
and together we can talk,
and chat, and ponder,
about life, the universe,
and what the difference is
between a gherkin and a cucumber.

TODAY'S SPECIAL

Are you listening?

Acts 2:14, 36-41: Peter speaks to the crowd

Equipment:
flipchart
pen
music and lyrics

This activity should possibly come with a health warning! Write the word 'CHURCH' on the flipchart. Ask the group how they could make church unattractive, boring, a turn-off, irrelevant and uninviting. In other words, how could they stop people coming to church (or not want to attend in the first place!).

Write the group's responses on the left-hand side of the page. Now, take each of the responses and, on the right-hand side of the page, write the opposite to the original response. For instance, if someone suggested 'preach for hours', then the opposite would be: 'short, sharp talks'.

See how you go, but don't feel offended if some of the group's initial responses are all too familiar to your church!

(Allow 10 minutes for this activity)

Church can sometimes appear friendly and warm, and at other times be cold and make you feel solitary.

Have a look at 'The Holy Spirit is here' (*The source 2*, 982/*The Australian Worship Collection*, 99) or 'Every nation, power and tongue' (*The Australian Worship Collection*, 10).

(Allow 5 minutes for this)

What do the group think 'church' should be about?

Read Acts 2:14, 36-41.
The whole concept of 'church' can leave people baffled and bemused. What is the whole thing all about? Why do people put on some of their least creased clothes, wash behind their ears and go into a building to meet with similarly minimum-crease people?

A lot of questions arise the moment we consider the purpose of going to church. At times it may seem as if we're members of a club, or that we're propping up a sagging institution or even because there's not much to watch on TV on a Sunday morning. At these times it's worth revisiting the beginning of this whole church idea.

At the time that Peter spoke, Jerusalem was bulging with visitors for the Feast of Pentecost (also known as the Feast of Weeks). Jews from every corner of the known world had come to Jerusalem for this special occasion. Peter's speech must have been spoken against a backdrop of hustle and bustle, with the noise of hundreds of voices reverberating around the buildings.

The significant thing here is that even with all the noise and the main event of the festival, thousands of people stopped to listen to the ex-fisherman turned disciple.

A lot of the people must have known or heard of Jesus and that the Jewish authorities had labelled him a criminal. It must have also been common knowledge that this same Jesus had been crucified. But, somehow, the words of Peter cut through the general hubbub and made an impact on several thousand people.

The main part of Peter's message was that the people should change their hearts, ask God to forgive them and receive the Holy Spirit to enable them to live as God would want them to.

Almost immediately, over three thousand people had a common purpose and a new direction for living. This is what brought them together, this is what gave them a sense of purpose, and this is what caused them to want to share time together.

This is what should still give today's church its aim and the main purpose for everyone going to church.

Ask the group to suggest reasons why people go to church today. The reasons can either be their own, those of people they know or reasons that they may have heard or read about. List the reasons onto the flipchart.

(Allow 5 minutes for this task)

Draw a large square onto the flipchart and write the group's names in the square. Ask the group to look at all the names while you read the following prayer:

Lord,
    this church thing,
    is at best a bit odd,
    and at worst,
    the most boring time I've ever had to spend
    (apart from sitting through a documentary on painting ceilings).
But the funny thing is, Lord,
    that when you look around
    at all these bodies
    gathered in one place
    to chat about you,
    sing a bit,
    and listen to the vicar
    try and tell a joke,
    without giving away the punchline,
    or forget he was telling a joke
    in the first place.
Then,
    when we're having a cup of tea,
    and a biscuit if some little grubby fingers haven't nicked them all,
    there seems to be an odd assortment of people
    who, for one reason or another,
    want to know more about you.
And, Lord,
    I'm really glad
    that you love
    every size, shape, colour, texture and hue,
    and you don't care one little bit
    about status, prestige, earnings, cars,
    gadgets or designer clothes,
    because you care about the person,
    the body inside
    which is vulnerable, sensitive and needs
    a lot of TLC.
So, thanks,
    thanks that you love me, and him, and her
    and every single fragile human being,
    wherever and whatever, amen.

TODAY'S SPECIAL

Give a little bit
Acts 2:42-47: Life among the Lord's followers

Equipment:
pen and paper for each group member
music and lyrics
fireproof container
matches

Give each member of the group a pen and a piece of paper. Ask them to think about one possession that means more to them than anything else they own. Write the item onto the piece of paper, fold the paper in half and place the collected papers onto a table or other surface. Shuffle the papers and select one at random. Read the item to the group and they must decide whether to keep the item or get rid of it. Hopefully, the person who owns the item in question will try and persuade the rest of the group to keep it. Repeat the process with all the other items until you have reduced the number of 'kept' items. The object is to reduce the number of items until there is just one item left which the group have agreed to keep.

- What are the reasons for keeping this one remaining item?
- Is everyone agreed about this item?
- Was the process of getting rid of the other items difficult?

(Allow 10 minutes for this activity)

Our possessions mean a lot to each of us. Being asked to give some things away is extremely hard. Take a look at 'We bow down' (*The source 2*, 1028) or 'When the cares of life come' (*The source 2*, 1055).

(Allow 5 minutes for this)

Is it really possible to feel that possessions are unimportant?

Read Acts 2:42-47.
We live in a society, and a world as a whole, where private possessions are important. We are often assessed according to what we own. Our friends sometimes look to see what clothes we wear and whether they're

an 'acceptable' label. Young children usually argue about having the biggest, tallest, strongest, most colourful toy, while adults can look either envious or smug about the car they and other people drive. Possessions are used as a measure of success. This kind of living will always have winners and losers.

At the time Peter spoke, the Lord's followers would have been a mixture of wealthy and poor, educated and illiterate people who represented a cross-section of humanity. As an expression of God's love, and to reinforce the idea of God's love being equally for all, Peter and the other Apostles encouraged everyone to share what they had to make sure that no one felt left out or on the fringes.

This style of living made an impression on everyone who knew or heard about the early Christians. Their belief and faith in God wasn't based upon a set of laws or rituals but on developing a lifestyle that was a true reflection of their change of heart.

Having possessions isn't wrong, it's the attitude of our heart that's the deciding factor. If we consider our possessions to be more important than the welfare and health of other people, then perhaps we should begin to question what we place our trust in?

Ask the group to list a number of their possessions according to their priority. For example, the most important item may be a piece of jewellery, followed by a TV, then a bike, CD player and so on. You could suggest that they place the items on a scale of 1-10.

(Allow 5 minutes for this task)

Ask each member of the group to place their list in the container. Take a match and set light to the pieces of paper. It might be advised to have a jug of water near by . . . just in case.

While the paper burns/smoulders read the following:

Proverbs 2:3-7, 9-11

I wanted to find out what was best for us during this short time we have on this earth. So I decided to make myself happy with wine and find out what it means to be foolish, without really being foolish myself. I did some great things. I built houses and planted vineyards. I had flower gardens and orchards full of fruit trees. And I had pools where I could get water for the trees. I owned slaves, and their sons and daughters became my slaves. I had more sheep and goats than anyone who had ever lived in Jerusalem . . . I got whatever I wanted and did whatever made me happy. But most of all I enjoyed hard work. Then I thought about everything I had done, including the hard work, and it was simply chasing the wind. Nothing on earth is worth the trouble.

TODAY'S SPECIAL

Ouch!
Acts 7:55-60: Stephen is stoned to death

Equipment:
cards
music and lyrics
short piece of string for each group member

Hand out the cards with the sentences below:

- The monkey escaped but . . .
- When Aunt Ethel saw the mess she . . .
- Dad went absolutely ballistic when he saw the car but . . .
- If I ever see him/her again I'll . . .
- The doctor said that it'd be OK in a few years' time so I said . . .
- When I woke up and saw what had happened I . . .
- It wasn't so much the money but the fact that she'd painted my feet pink. When I see her I'll . . .

You might like to think of other slightly wacky scenarios. The idea is for the group member to read the sentence and conclude the story which *must* include the word 'forgiveness' somewhere. It doesn't necessarily mean that the story concludes with someone being forgiven. Encourage the group to let their imaginations run riot.

(Allow 10 minutes for this activity)

Forgiveness isn't just a big word, it's a big deal!

Have a look at 'You love me as you found me' (*The Australian Worship Collection*, 131) or 'Whenever I see your face' (*The Australian Worship Collection*, 122).

(Allow 5 minutes for this)

Ask the group how they feel when someone apologises to them or simply says 'sorry.'

Read Acts 7:55-60.
The stoning of Stephen is a horrific story. Simply because the council leaders objected strongly to what Stephen had to say (see verse 54 which suggests that they were absolutely furious), the leaders dragged him out of the city and, without a legal trial, they killed him.

Stephen must have known that there was no escape from this situation; death was to be the only outcome. However, expecting the worst, Stephen didn't cringe or try to dodge the stones, instead he knelt down and shouted to God to forgive those who were attempting to kill him!

Such an act of forgiveness may seem extraordinary and quite beyond any of us. However, it's surprising how difficult we find it to forgive, or apologise, for the simplest of things. By refusing to put things right with someone, we are allowing the situation to become worse and sour everything we do. The situation eats away at our minds and colours the way we see and think.

By choosing to deal with the situation, we are allowing something of God's love to enter and encourage us to put the hassle behind us and look forward to the rest of the day with a clear mind.

Sometimes we cannot deal directly with the person, or people, responsible for the hassle, but we can let it be known that we refuse to add fuel to the flames and choose to forgive whatever needs forgiveness. Some people may suggest that it's being weak to forgive yet it's surprising what does happen when we choose to use the power of forgiveness.

Discuss situations where the group have been faced with a dilemma over whether to forgive or look for revenge. Has revenge made the situation better or worse? Has forgiveness made any difference?
(Allow 5 minutes for this task)

Give everyone a piece of string. Ask them to tie as many knots in the string as they possibly can. When they have finished explain that unresolved situations can become like knots. They tie up our thoughts, our emotions and our actions until we are nothing more than a collection of knots. Ask the group to hold their piece of knotted string while you read the following prayer:

Lord,
  I know it's the right thing to do,
  this forgiveness bit.
But surely,
  if I go about forgiving everybody
  won't they just keep on
  doing what they did in the first place,
  and annoy me something rotten?
Yet, I suppose the idea
  is not just to say
  'I forgive you',
  but do something practical,
  like smacking them in the mouth!
OK, only joking,
  but that might make me feel better for an instant,
  until they smack me in the mouth,
  and then we've got two sore mouths
  instead of two talking mouths
  who've decided to deal with the situation
  rather than provide more reasons
  to get smacked in the mouth!
It seems to me
  that forgiveness
  is more action than words,
  even though words are extremely useful
  when trying to persuade the other person
  that violence tends to make me wince
  in pain.
Lord,
  thank you,
  that the greatest act of forgiveness
  resulted in Jesus being crucified,
  and dying so that all my irrational behaviour
  and corruption
  is dealt with, for ever.
Now, on an easier note,
  can you help me deal with this rather irritating person . . . me!

TODAY'S SPECIAL   **To whom it may concern**
Acts 17:22-31: Paul in Athens

Equipment:
pen and paper for each group member
music and lyrics
Bible

This is a simple exercise, which might (not guaranteed) make you appear really cool to the group.

Give the group a pen and piece of paper each and ask them to think of a number and then write it onto the piece of paper. Insist that they show no one the number or tell anyone. Now, ask them to double the original number, multiply it by five, and then write the total at the bottom of the piece of paper.

Select any person in the group and ask them to tell you the total written at the bottom of their paper. Within moments you will be able to tell them their original number.

The trick is to take off the last digit of the number they give you. For example: if the original number is 26, doubling it gives 52, then multiplying by five gives you 260. Simply take away the zero and you have the original number. Neat, eh?

(Allow 10 minutes for this activity)

People are often either impressed or totally fazed by what they don't understand or which appears to be beyond their experience.

Take a look at 'Among the gods' (*The source*, 19/*The British Worship Collection*, 8) or 'This is the best place' (*The British Worship Collection*, 98).

(Allow 5 minutes for this)

The words to the songs are positive and directed at God who we know loves us. Can you imagine composing lyrics to some unknown god of whom you have no knowledge or experience?

Read Acts 17:22-31.
Paul is in Athens, which is acknowledged as being a great city, famed for its philosophers and academics. It was just as famous for its temples,

statues and monuments. A legend of Athens describes a horrific disease which swept through the city. All attempts to appease the gods and halt the disease met with no success. A wise man of the city took a flock of sheep to the top of a hill and released them. Wherever the sheep stopped, an altar was erected and dedicated to an anonymous 'god', and the animal was sacrificed there and then. It is said that the spread of the disease was halted immediately.

Paul, in his speech, states that he considers the people of Athens to be very religious, particularly with all these unknown gods to worship. Having said that, he then goes on to describe the living God who gave, and gives, life to every living thing. Paul stresses that God isn't made of materials dug from the earth, or confined to fancy buildings, but a God who wishes to get to know each person as an individual, to get on personal terms with everyone.

Even today, we can place our trust and faith in objects, or perform superstitious rituals, in an attempt to ensure that life turns out the way we would like it to. Yet the living God is waiting to welcome each one of us and to care for every detail of our life, not as in some trade off for our performing a series of tasks or rituals, but freely, having paid the price for us through the death and resurrection of Jesus Christ.

We don't have to place our trust in inanimate objects but in a God who wants to be with us each step of our life's journey.

Ask the group to list as many forms of superstition as they can. What kinds of superstitious acts do people perform for 'good luck'?

Discuss these and whether they really make a difference to the outcome of an event.

(Allow 5 minutes for this task)

Place the Bible in the centre of the room. Ask the group to gather around the Bible and, if they want to participate, to place their hand on the Bible. Explain that the one definite fact we have is that what God says he will do for us is a certainty. The Bible contains examples and references to many of the ways in which God has done exactly what he said he will do. This is the kind of God who we should trust our life with. In a moment of quiet, read the following:

Psalm 25:1-5
I offer you my heart, Lord God, and I trust you.
Don't make me ashamed or let enemies defeat me.
Don't disappoint any of your worshippers,
    but disappoint all deceitful liars.
Show me your paths and teach me to follow;
    guide me by your truth and instruct me.
You keep me safe, and I always trust you.

TODAY'S SPECIAL

Keep your chin up!
Acts 1:6-14: Jesus is taken to heaven

Equipment:
tubes of toothpaste
plastic cups
towels
music and lyrics

Ask for three or four pairs of volunteers. Have one of the volunteers lay on the floor, face up, with the plastic cup held in their mouth. Spread the towel over their chest and shoulders. The partner stands over them and, without stooping or bending, attempts to empty the toothpaste into the cup.

A simple, fun game which might require some sort of prize to make the whole game worth while.

(Allow 10 minutes for this activity)

Some things in life are simply for fun while others take some thinking about!

Take a look at 'Holy Spirit, rain down' (*The source 2*, 745) or 'The Holy Spirit is here' (*The source 2*, 982).

(Allow 5 minutes for this)

Ask the group what they thought of the lyrics to the chosen song.

Read Acts 1:6-14.
The disciples, now called apostles, had become used to having Jesus around again. It wasn't long before that they'd witnessed Jesus being crucified and buried and had lost all hope of God establishing any form of kingdom on earth. Now, they were anxious for Jesus to at last do the right thing and set himself up as the true King of Israel.

The apostles expected Jesus to reply with a precise date, or at least give them a rough idea within the next couple of weeks. Instead, Jesus replied that his return wasn't to be known by anyone and that they shouldn't concern themselves with the details! You can imagine the look on several faces.

Jesus goes on to tell them that the Holy Spirit will be theirs and give them power to go out and tell everyone the good news of Jesus Christ. As they were watching and listening, Jesus was surrounded by a cloud, which lifted him heavenwards. While the apostles were watching with open mouths, two men, dressed in white, asked why they were looking into the sky? Jesus had been taken to heaven.

The apostles must have felt completely let down, precisely the opposite to Jesus! Losing Jesus once was more than they could bear and, after his resurrection, they'd become confident that he'd be around for a long while. But now he'd disappeared again, and this time it seemed to be for good!

Jesus had already told the apostles that the Holy Spirit would be with them even when he wasn't. But this promise seemed difficult to appreciate when Jesus had been removed from their presence again. Rather than become depressed, the apostles returned to Jerusalem and decided to pray to God and wait for something to happen.

All too often we can look at the situation before us and feel that everything is beyond our comprehension. However, by following the apostles' example, it is always better to chat with God about things before we descend into a state of misery.

Ask the group how they would have felt if they had been the apostles watching Jesus disappear.

- What would their feelings have been?
- What would have been their initial reaction?
- Would they have gone their separate ways rather than keep together?
- Is it easier to place our faith in things we can see and touch rather than that which is unseen?

(Allow 5 minutes for this task)

Give each group member a piece of paper and a pen, and ask them to write down any questions that they may have concerning the Holy Spirit. Tell them that you will attempt to answer each of their questions over the next few weeks.

Collect the questions and ask the group to be still for a few moments while you read the following:

2 Timothy 1:9-10

God saved us and chose us to be his holy people. We did nothing to deserve this, but God planned it because he is so kind, even before time began God planned for Christ Jesus to show kindness to us. Now Christ Jesus has come to show us the kindness of God. Christ our Saviour defeated death and brought us the good news. It shines like a light and offers life that never ends.

TODAY'S SPECIAL

Connected!
Acts 2:1-21: The coming of the Holy Spirit

Equipment:
postcard for each member of the group
music and lyrics
sticky tape
notepaper
pens
candle

On each postcard write *one* letter and *one* word, which begins with the same letter of the alphabet. Either allow each group member to select a card at random (have the cards face down), or tape a card under each seat. If the group is fairly small, simply ask them to get their cards and try to make as many words as possible. This is done in the following way. Firstly, the group should look at their combined words and see what sort of sentence they can make using the words only (not all of the cards have to be used). They may not be able to make a complete, or sensible, sentence with the words they've got. This is where the single letters come into play. Once the group have decided on a sentence, they can then see what word/s they can make from the letters, which can then be included in the sentence.

If the group is large enough, give each member of the group a number. Call out a sequence of random numbers and those members must try and form a sentence using their words and letters.

There are some variations of the above game. You can ask the group to firstly make a word using the letters and then combine this word into a sentence that is made with the other words on the cards. Alternatively, have the words on one set of cards and the single letters on another set. Give out the words first and ask the group to make a sentence. Then give out the single letter cards and make a word from these letters. Once they have done this ask the group to include the new word in the sentence which they have previously made.

(Allow 10 minutes for this activity)

Ask the group what they thought was difficult about the game. Have a look at 'Holy Spirit, I surrender' (*The Australian Worship Collection Book 2*, 26) or 'I believe' (*The Australian Worship Collection Book 2*, 29).

(Allow 5 minutes for this)

Have you ever thought how much we depend upon electricity for our daily lives?

Read Acts 2:1-21.

Each day our actions, from morning to night, depend upon having energy. Initially, we need the physical energy to propel ourselves (or crawl) out of bed, amble to the bathroom, show our face at the mirror and then slither downstairs towards a bowl of cereal. After that the whole day is one chaotic jumble of movement which, hopefully, results in performing the right actions at the right time.

However, although we require our physical energy to move around, we are also totally dependent upon other forms of energy to help us complete both simple and complex tasks throughout each day.

Simple functions, such as heating water, light, communication, each require an energy form to work. This energy isn't a secret or hidden power source. We know of its existence, we understand, basically, how it is made and how it works, and we know of its effects on our daily lives. The energy is something we usually take for granted and simply expect it to be there when we need it. But, when that energy source isn't available, even for a short time, we feel isolated, frustrated and deprived.

In the reading, we find the Lord's followers meeting together in Jerusalem not really sure what the future held for them. They had no idea how they could fulfil what Jesus had asked them to do when he told them to 'go to the people of all nations and make them my disciples, baptise them in the name of the Father, the Son and the Holy Spirit' (see Matthew 28:19).

Without warning, and totally unexpected, on the day of Pentecost, the Lord's followers were given an energy source which would give them the power to perform all that Jesus had asked of them. The Lord's followers, and countless others, now knew that God was going to be with them wherever they went. They knew they could depend upon God, that he keeps his promises and that he wouldn't ask them to do anything without giving them the right power source.

This same power source also provides us with the strength that we need to work through the questions and hassles that confront us each day.

Give the group a piece of notepaper and a pen and ask them to identify some of the things that they don't understand or their apprehension at allowing God to have a say in their life.

Collect the notes together.

(Allow 5 minutes for this task)

Place a candle in the centre of the room. Light the candle and place all the notes around the base of the candle. Ask the group to be quiet while you read the following prayer:

Lord,
    I feel,
    well, I am a bit,
    no, hang on,
    more than a bit,
    something approximate to a large brick building,
    apprehensive, and even a touch frightened,
    about allowing you to deal with things in my life.
It's not that I don't trust you,
    you understand,
    it's just that, I sort of, well,
    can't quite get my head around
    having someone else
    saying what they think about,
    and suggesting alternative types of behaviour,
    for my actions.
From what I understand,
    it's not a one-off sort of thing;
    you seem to imply
    that you want to get involved
    on a daily basis!
Now, that's a lot of involvement
    for someone like you,
    with someone like me.
I'm not sure what you want from me,
    or what I'm supposed to be doing
    or not doing!
But, whatever it is,
    I know I'm never going to find out
    by shutting myself away
    in my emotional dustbin.
So, I suppose,
    even though I might regret saying this later
    (or, if it turns out OK, maybe I won't regret it!),
    I think it might be about time
    that we joined forces,
    and faced the world,
    together.
And that you'll be my power source,
    when all around me seems

daunting and confusing.
That you'll be my friend
   when loneliness strikes,
   that you'll stick up for me
   against the giants of fear, anger and hurt
   that try to trample all over me.
Be with me, Lord,
   when my eyes are open,
   and when they're closed.
Be with me.

28

TODAY'S SPECIAL

And now for the goodbyes
2 Corinthians 13:11-13: Final greetings

Equipment:
paper and pen for each group member
music and lyrics

Distribute the paper and pens to the group. Ask each member to write on the paper one fact about themselves that no one else in the group knows. For instance, 'When I was four, my brother pushed a piece of soap into my mouth because I called him a camel' or 'When I was six my mum made me have dancing lessons and I had to dress up as an apple at the Christmas show.' Tell the group not to write their name on the piece of paper.

After everyone has completed writing their 'fact', collect the papers and read one out at a time and see if the rest of the group can guess who it is.

(Allow 10 minutes for this activity)

Usually, only good friends know about some areas of our life that we may not want to be made public.

Take a look at 'Lord, you have my heart' (*The source*, 341) or 'To be in your presence' (*The source*, 524).

(Allow 5 minutes for this)

Ask the group to have a look at the lyrics to the chosen song. Do the words say anything in particular?

Read 2 Corinthians 13:11-13.
What is the definition of a friend? Would you agree that a friend is: 'Someone who you're not embarrassed to be yourself with?' or could it be: 'Someone who makes me feel totally accepted?'

Friendship is one of the greatest gifts anyone can give to another person. There are possibly many people who we might consider to be 'sort of' friends or just acquaintances, but friends who you can rely on whatever the situation, are often few and very precious.

Often friendship develops over a long period of time, where you slowly get to know each other and become confident in sharing little bits about yourself. There are always those people who will listen to what you have to say and then, before you know it, every single detail is broadcast on the evening news!

Friends are people who you are not afraid to make a mistake in front of. They are the sort of people who will support you and stick up for you against all the odds. Friends should be the type of people who won't be afraid to be honest with you, such as when you say: 'Do I look OK wearing this?' and they reply: 'Erm, you sort of look like something that should be entered for a dog show!'

To have a real friend, and to be a real friend to someone is something that is extremely precious. It helps get us through stages in our life that are tough and best not faced alone. Being friendly to other people is also an encouragement and helps to make them feel accepted and not as if they've just arrived from some distant planet.

Paul's final greetings to the Corinthian church encourages honesty, openness, acceptance and kindness. These are all traits that we should encourage in each other and especially with those people who we consider to be real, close friends.

Divide the group into smaller groups. Ask them to consider the idea of 'friends' and get them to write some definitions of 'friendship'. Once they've all finished, share the results with everyone.

(Allow 5 minutes for this task)

Place the definitions of 'friendship' on the walls or notice board. Ask the group to think about their friends, or lack of them, while you read the following:

Proverbs 27:5-10, 17
A truly good friend will openly correct you. You can trust a friend who corrects you, but kisses from an enemy are nothing but lies. If you have had enough to eat, honey doesn't taste good, but if you are really hungry you will eat anything. When you are far from home, you feel like a bird without a nest. The sweet smell of incense can make you feel good, but true friendship is better still. Don't desert an old friend of your family or visit your relatives when you are in trouble. A friend nearby is better than relatives far away . . . just as iron sharpens iron, friends sharpen the minds of each other.

TODAY'S SPECIAL   **Sounds good!**
Psalm 34:1-10: Honour the Lord

Equipment:
photocopied sheets
pens
music and lyrics
large sheet of paper

Copy the test paper below onto a master sheet and photocopy sufficient to have one sheet per person.

Give each group member a copy of the 'test' and a pen.

TEST

Instructions: Answer each question in order. If you are unable to answer any question, pass on to the next question and, if you have time, go back to the question. Read through all the questions before attempting the test.

1. Write your name in the top right-hand corner of the paper.
2. Print your address on the left-hand side of the paper.
3. Circle the correct answer:

   a. The tomato is a: vegetable, mineral, fruit?
   b. Paris is the capital of: Germany, France, Italy?
   c. Lira is the currency of: Austria, Belgium, Italy?

4. Raise your right hand to inform the group leader that you have completed the first three questions. When they nod you can continue with the test.
5. True or false? (tick the correct answer)

   a. Uranus is visible to the naked eye.   T/F
   b. The diameter of the moon is 3,476km.   T/F
   c. Antarctic means 'opposite' of the Arctic.   T/F

6. Is this word spelt correctly: 'Constantinople'. Yes/No
7. Stand up until the group leader tells you to sit down.
8. What is the opposite of 'Lethargy'?
9 What is the missing number from the following sequence: 5, 7, 11, 13, ? 17?
10. You should have read through the entire test paper before answering. Do not answer questions 1-9. Write your name at the top of the

sheet and then remain quiet until the group leader declares the test over.

(Allow 10 minutes for this activity)

How did the members of the group feel when they were told that they shouldn't have attempted any of the test questions? Sometimes we 'jump' into situations and then feel really annoyed when it is made clear that we have wasted our time!

Take a look at 'Lord, my heart before you' (*The source 2*, 875) or 'It's all for you' (*The source 2*, 805).

(Allow 5 minutes for this)

Ask the group whether they feel it is necessary to regularly say thank you to God?

Read Psalm 34:1-10.
Verses 1-10 of this psalm can be divided into three distinctive parts.

Firstly, the psalmist states that we should continually thank God for loving us, being there whenever we need him and to offer our 'praise' (to commend or speak highly of). The usual idea is that we should only thank God when things are OK, going right or when something has turned out just the way we want it to! However, here, the psalmist is insisting that we offer praise to God at *all* times. It is quite easy to give God a big thank-you when a good thing has occurred, or when we've just come out of a regular check-up with the dentist and there are no problems! It's quite another thing to offer our praise to God when things are gloomy or everything seems to be against us.

Secondly, the psalmist is telling us that all those people who continually look to God, whatever the situation, will never be disappointed. The 'but' here is that our disappointment may be the case of asking for, or expecting God to do things that are not really the best things for us. It's important to make sure that we remember to keep in touch with him (reading the Bible and praying) so that when we suggest that he might like to do this or that for us, our requests don't go against what he has already said should happen.

Thirdly, we should share our experiences of God. It's always good to hear how God has worked with other people and what has happened as a result. This is not so that we should mumble that God would never do anything 'like that' with us, but to be encouraged that he loves us so much that he wants to be involved with every detail of our life.

Offering our praise to God isn't like uttering a 'good luck' charm or trusting in a superstition; saying thank you to God begins with a genuine gratitude that God takes delight in being with us and loves us unreservedly. Whenever we start from that point then everything else tends to fall into place.

Ask the group to suggest situations where they believe God has made a real difference. It doesn't matter how insignificant the experience, all are a possible encouragement to other people.

(Allow 5 minutes for this task)

Write the following acrostic onto the large sheet of paper. Explain what each letter represents and then ask the group to reflect on the word.

P: praise . . . to commend or speak highly of.

R: remembering . . . what God has done for us and for others.

A: always . . . continually chat with God.

Y: yearning . . . the desire to chat with God and share our life with him.

E: everything . . . don't leave out any areas of our life.

R: recognising . . . that God doesn't care what we chat about and never expects us to restrict our prayers to the good times.

While the group are quiet, read the following:

1 Thessalonians 5:14-16
My friends, we beg you to warn anyone who isn't living right. Encourage anyone who feels left out, help all who are weak, and be patient with everyone. Don't be hateful to people, just because they are hateful to you. Rather, be good to each other and to everyone else. Always be joyful and never stop praying.

TODAY'S SPECIAL

In trouble, again!
Psalm 43: A prayer in times of trouble

Equipment:
postcards
blindfolds
chairs
music and lyrics

Write one of the following instructions onto each postcard.

Turn left one step
Turn right one step
Go forward one step
Go backwards one step
Go forward two steps
Go backwards two steps

Have several copies of each instruction. Invite one member of the group to be blindfolded. Stand them in the centre of the room. Place a number of chairs around the room randomly. Shuffle the cards and ask one member of the group to take one card and read it aloud. The blindfolded member of the group must do exactly what the card tells them to do. Invite a second member of the group to pick another card and read it, again the blindfolded member follows the instructions.

Repeat the process until all the cards are used up or the blindfolded member cannot go any further. If the group member reaches a wall or door, take another card until one of them gives an opportunity to move away from the obstacle.

You can make this game more fun/difficult by having two or three blindfolded members starting at different points of the room, each responding to the same card.

(Allow 10 minutes for this activity)

Ask the blindfolded group members what it was like to receive instructions and not be able to see where they were going. Ask other members of the group what it was like to see the obstacles and not be able to do anything other than what was stated on the cards.

Take a look at 'O, draw me, Lord' (*The American Worship Collection,* 62) or 'You are here' (*The American Worship Collection,* 107).

(Allow 5 minutes for this)

Is it really possible that God wants to be with us even when life stinks?

Read Psalm 43.

The psalmist begins by showing how he feels that everyone is against him and that nothing he does is right. At first, the psalmist says that he feels as if even God has deserted him, but rather than run away and hide or moan at God for letting the situation happen in the first place, he tells God that there is nowhere else to go but to him.

Light and truth are the two things asked for which the psalmist acknowledges as being the only items which can bring any peace. Once this is recognised and the author of the psalm begins to praise God, then he begins to question why he felt so desperate in the first place! The whole thing changes from a statement of despair to one of encouragement and hope.

This psalm offers everyone a straightforward guide to dealing with whatever life throws at us. It may appear simplistic, but it offers an effective three-part approach to dealing with any situation: 'God, this is how I see things at the moment' and 'I don't know what to do but you do, please show me' through to 'you're the only one who can help me, thank you.'

That's something to remember whenever we feel as if life has dumped a load of the unexpected on us!

One of the best ways of developing our relationship with God is to learn more about his thoughts and ways. We can learn from other people how God has helped them in their life and, more importantly, we can learn about God from the Bible.

Often, the best way to do this is to find somewhere that's quiet and you won't be interrupted, and to read a short piece from the Bible. Ask God to help you understand what you have just read and see how it could apply to your life.

The game that the group played earlier demonstrates how, when we can't see where we are going, it is important to have help to guide us through. The Bible is an important guide for us every day.

Ask the group to look at Psalm 119:105. Give them a few moments to think about the reading and then ask the question: 'What does this mean?'

Allow 5 minutes for this task.

Ask the group to reflect on what their responses were to the previous question. Suggest that they spend a few moments in quiet while you read the following:

Psalm 70:5
I am poor and needy,
    but you, the Lord God, care about me.
You are the one who saves me.
Please hurry and help!

TODAY'S SPECIAL

Help!
Psalm 70: God is wonderful!

Equipment:
postcards
pen and paper for each group member
large sheet of paper in the shape of a question mark
music and lyrics

Give each group member a piece of paper and a pen. Read one of the 'problems' from the postcards (have the 'problems' (below) written prior to the session). Ask the group to write on their piece of paper what their response would be. After you have posed all the 'problems' ask the group to discuss the issues as a whole, and attempt to arrive at a group response for each 'problem'.

Problems:

1. You have just discovered that your best friend is cheating on their partner. Help! What do you do?

2. You are browsing in a charity shop and find a twenty-pound note on the floor. Help! What do you do?

3. A friend has given you a computer disk containing a copy of an assignment, which you haven't done any work for. The assignment is due in tomorrow. Help! What do you do?

4. It's late, there's not a lot of people or traffic around. One of your mates offers to let you have a drive of their car even though you're too young to drive. Help! What do you do?

5. The restaurant is busy and the waiter has miscalculated your bill. You are being asked to pay ten pounds less than you should be charged. Help! What do you do?

6. Your dad has loaned you his mobile phone because you have run out of credit on your phone. He tells you to use it only in an emergency. You've got loads of friends who you need to call or text. Help! What do you do?

7. Your brother let you borrow his portable mini-disc player. You left it on the table while you had a drink of orange and, somehow, spilt juice all over his mini-disc player. You've wiped off as much of the juice as you can but the disc player doesn't seem to work properly. Help! What do you do?

8. A wrinkled relative has given you a hand-knitted, multicoloured scarf for your birthday. Even your mum can't suppress a giggle. The relative is expecting you to wear the scarf the next time you visit. Help! What do you do?

9. A friend has drawn some pictures of a teacher, which are very funny but are likely to humiliate the teacher. The pictures have begun to appear all over school. Help! What do you do?

10. You've managed to put some blue dye into the shower-head in the bathroom. The joke is intended for your brother but your mum has gone into the bathroom to have a shower first. Help! What do you do?

The group discussion should not attempt to find the 'right' solution to the problem, but agree as a group about what they really would do in that situation.

Ask the group to fold their pieces of paper and pin them to the paper 'question mark', which can then be placed on the wall.

(Allow 10 minutes for this activity)

Lots of situations cause us to stop and think about what would be the best thing to do. Often, it's never clear whether your chosen course of action was the best after all. Have a look at 'Create in me a pure heart' (*The source 2*, 670) or 'Lord, my heart before you' (*The source 2*, 875).

(Allow 5 minutes for this)

Knowing what's right to do isn't always the easiest thing to do.

Read Psalm 70.

This psalm seems to have been written in a hurry. It's as if something has suddenly exploded and the writer is in desperate need of help.

We have a clue as to the nature of the problems. It appears that the psalmist is being threatened by people who want to kill him, some people who want to rearrange his face, and other, so-called, 'friends' who are mocking him and saying 'We told you so'.

In Psalm 70, the writer doesn't seem to have either the time or energy to go into long, drawn-out explanations for his actions, or why things have turned out the way that they have. Rather, he gets straight to the point and says, 'God, if you don't do something to help me, I might not get to see another sunrise!'

At times, we can also feel in a desperate state, when nothing else seems more important than dealing with a huge mountain of hassle that threatens to bury us. There is absolutely nothing wrong in crying out to God and asking him to deal with the situation . . . double quick.

It might be that we wouldn't get into certain situations that threaten to wipe the smile off our faces if we had spent a little more time chatting to God in the first place. Chatting doesn't ensure that we never get into scrapes, but it might just give us a clue how to act or react at the crucial time.

Ask each member of the group to take their piece of paper from the question-mark-shaped piece of paper. Suggest that they might like to write about one situation which is giving them grief at the moment. Ask them to look at Psalm 62:8, and to put their own name before the verse, making it personal to them. For example: 'John, trust God, my friend, and always tell him each one of your concerns. God is your place of safety.'

(Allow 5 minutes for this task)

Ask the group to hold their piece of paper in their cupped hands while you read the following prayer:

Lord,
    how on earth do I stop feeling
    screwed up, washed up, tied up,
    scrunched up, fed up, messed up,
    and dried up,
    without allowing all my bodily functions
    to stop working?
Because, Lord, you've got to admit,
    I do a really good imitation of a wreck,
    without a rehearsal.
It's not that I go out of my way
    to make a complete
    donkey of myself,
    it's just that some things
    are natural!
When I'm threatened,
    and mocked,
    I must try to wise up, and remember

that some people
are a bit touchy at times
and that it's far better to talk to you
than listen to a load of monkeys talking bananas.
So, Lord,
I'm not saying that even sharing my thoughts with you
is going to guarantee that I won't put my foot
where it isn't wanted,
but at least I'm really glad to know
that you're always with me
and would prefer a quick yelp of help
than a long silence which ends in ouch!

TODAY'S SPECIAL   ## For ever and a bit longer
Psalm 90:1-8, 12: God is eternal

Equipment:
small jigsaw puzzle for each group (you could make these by cutting up old birthday cards or Christmas cards)
plastic bags
music and lyrics

Divide the group into groups of 3 or 4. Remove each jigsaw from its container and place it into a plastic bag. Give each group one of the jigsaws and ask them to put the jigsaw together with the picture face down. They are not allowed to look at the picture or attempt to put the jigsaw together using the picture side and then turn the completed puzzle over!

Once the groups have finished (or given up!), ask them what it felt like to have nothing to refer to when trying to complete the jigsaw.

(Allow 10 minutes for this activity)

Without something to guide our actions, things can get pretty tough.

Take a look at 'Praise the name of Jesus' (*The source*, 435/*The American Worship Collection*, 76) or 'You loved me' (*The American Worship Collection*, 113).

(Allow 5 minutes for this)

Ask the group whether they think that the chosen song provides a sort of reference point or guidelines?

Read Psalm 90:1-8, 12.
It's only someone who's a few fries short of a happy meal who'd walk into a foreign landscape without a map and a compass. Even with all the equipment available and advice on where to go and not to go, people still get lost and require a rescue team to find them and bring them to safety.

Even people who've found themselves in an alien environment through an accident still believe that they can take on the landscape and win!

Very few people would accept the challenge of scaling a mountain, sailing an ocean, doing mole impressions underground or trekking across a continent without guides who know every intimate detail of the terrain and are skilled in surviving whatever the weather can throw at them. Most people who take on a challenge want to know that they stand a pretty good chance of surviving to tell the tale!

We all feel confident when we know precisely where we are. Without thinking about it, we are usually able to say exactly where we are at any given moment. If we are in an area that is unfamiliar to us, we make sure that we take a note of landmarks or street names so that we can at least have a guess as to our location if we were asked.

Our lives are based upon knowing where we are or where we are supposed to be. If we don't know where we are or where we are supposed to be, then it's quite probable that we're lost! If we visit a new place then we are often greeted by a map on a notice board which states clearly 'You are here!'. Our maps have reference points which enable us to work out where we are and where we want to go.

The psalmist understands our need to feel confident of our location when he acknowledges God as always being with us and as being our home. It could be said that the greatest challenge that we face is life itself. And, just as we prefer to know where we are, the psalmist refers to God as being our reference point.

God is constant. He doesn't shift about or change according to the weather. God knows what life is all about and he understands every single aspect of living. There is nothing that God isn't aware of or doesn't know how to deal with. He has provided a map (the Bible) and offered a guide (the Holy Spirit) to help us survive the greatest challenge. It'd be a shame to ignore them!

Ask the group to list all the things that require a reference book or guidelines for use. The list should be fairly extensive. Almost everything we buy comes with an instruction manual or guidelines.

Do these booklets or manuals have any value?

Why do we sometimes ignore the manuals?

(Allow 5 minutes for this task)

Suggest to the group that they might like to close their eyes and picture a desert or jungle landscape. Imagine how they would feel if they hadn't a clue as to where they were or where to go next. After a few moments, read the following:

Psalm 16:7-8
I praise you, Lord, for being my guide.
Even in the darkest night,
    your teachings fill my mind.
I will always look to you,
    as you stand beside me and protect me from fear.

TODAY'S SPECIAL

Thanks!

Psalm 95:1-7: Worship and obey the Lord

Equipment:

large sheet of paper with the word 'ORPWISH' written in large letters

paper and pen for each person

music and lyrics

Split the group into pairs and give each pair a piece of paper and a pen. Challenge them to make as many words as they can from the letters on the sheet.

Did anyone manage to make the word 'worship' out of the letters? If not, rewrite the letters to read 'WORSHIP'. Now ask the group to suggest definitions for the word. What do they think it means? Try to agree a short sentence which the group are happy with as a definition of worship.

(Allow 10 minutes for this activity)

The whole idea of worship is not an easy one to appreciate.

• Why do we worship?

• How do we worship?

• Does worship mean anything?

There are many questions and a lot of different responses which need sorting out.

Have a look at 'Lord, you have my heart' (*The source*, 341/*The British Worship Collection*, 61) or 'I will offer up my life' (*The British Worship Collection*, 42).

(Allow 5 minutes for this)

Do the words of the chosen song make the definition of worship any clearer?

Read Psalm 95:1-7.

Ask the group what they thought of the psalm. What do they think inspired the writer to say what he did?

If anyone is honest, they have said or thought that worship is a kind of happy, clappy, wimpy kind of thing that's best left to those people who've got nothing better to do with their lives than hop-skip-and-jump around the church.

The reality of worship, for the psalmist, is that it's a unique expression of a heart attitude. This doesn't mean that we can only express our gratitude towards God when we feel like we own the bank, or when we feel as sick as a room painted with every colour on a paint chart. Expressing how we feel is important to God. It doesn't matter whether we feel high, low or a bit in-between, it is important to tell God how we feel and show our appreciation that irrespective of our emotions, he loves us.

God is totally absorbed with us. He isn't fooled by the mask of indifference, or the polite smile which pretends life is OK. God loves getting involved in the nitty, gritty bits of our lives and likes nothing better than our honesty.

Expressing our heart towards God is an intimate part of our relationship with him. If you take a trip through the Psalms, you will find every human emotion on display. However, the psalmists never, ever tried to fool God and pretend life was a peach.

Worship is telling God that we're grateful he sticks by us, and also telling him why our life irritates us like a stone in our shoe at times. God loves our honesty. At least when we're chatting with him it means we're on speaking terms!

Give everyone a piece of paper and a pen. Ask them to write down some examples of times when they've felt really good and times when they've felt like a drain.

On the reverse of the paper, get the group to suggest some of the characteristics of God. For instance:

- he loves us
- he's always with us
- he'll never let us down
- he thinks I'm the best thing since marmalade on toast
- he protects me

(Allow 5 minutes for this task)

Once the group has finished writing some of their ideas about the characteristics of God, ask them to fold the paper and hold it in their hands. Ask them to think about some of their feelings over the last few weeks. While they are quiet, read the following:

Psalm 84:4-7, 11-12
You bless everyone who lives in your house,
    and they sing your praises.
You bless all who depend on you for their strength
    and all who deeply desire to visit your temple.
When they reach Dry Valley, springs start flowing,
    and the autumn rain fills it with pools of water.
Your people grow stronger,
    and you, the God of gods,
    will be seen in Zion . . .
    our Lord and our God,
    you are like the sun and also like a shield.
You treat us with kindness and with honour,
    never denying any good thing to those who live right.
Lord God, All-powerful,
    you bless everyone who trusts you.

BIBLE READING AND TOPIC INDEX

YEAR A

ADVENT

Unit 1	First Sunday of Advent	Matthew 24:36-44	The unexpected
Unit 2	Second Sunday of Advent	Matthew 3:1-12	Good news
Unit 3	Third Sunday of Advent	Matthew 11:2-11	Faith
Unit 4	Fourth Sunday of Advent	Matthew 1:18-25	Obedience

CHRISTMAS

Unit 5	First Sunday of Christmas	Matthew 2:13-23	Faith
Unit 6	Second Sunday of Christmas	John 1:1-9, 10-18	The Word

EPIPHANY

Unit 7	The Epiphany	Matthew 2:1-12	The wise men
Unit 8	First Sunday of Epiphany	Matthew 3:13-17	Baptism
Unit 9	Second Sunday of Epiphany	John 1:29-42	Salvation
Unit 10	Third Sunday of Epiphany	Matthew 4:12-23	Acceptance
Unit 11	Fourth Sunday of Epiphany	John 2:1-11	Miracles

LENT

Unit 12	Second Sunday before Lent	Matthew 6:25-34	Worry
Unit 13	Sunday next before Lent	Matthew 17:1-9	Fear
Unit 14	First Sunday of Lent	Matthew 4:1-11	Doubt
Unit 15	Second Sunday of Lent	John 3:1-17	Salvation
Unit 16	Third Sunday of Lent	John 4:5-42	Acceptance
Unit 17	Fourth Sunday of Lent	John 9:1-41	Healing
Unit 18	Fifth Sunday of Lent	John 11:1-45	Miracles
Unit 19	Palm Sunday	Matthew 21:1-11	Authority

EASTER

Unit 20	Easter Sunday	Matthew 28:1-10	Resurrection
Unit 21	Second Sunday of Easter	John 20:19-31	Evangelism
Unit 22	Third Sunday of Easter	Acts 2:14, 36-41	The Church
Unit 23	Fourth Sunday of Easter	Acts 2:42-47	God's love
Unit 24	Fifth Sunday of Easter	Acts 7:55-60	Faith
Unit 25	Sixth Sunday of Easter	Acts 17:22-31	Trust
Unit 26	Seventh Sunday of Easter	Acts 1:6-14	Perseverance
Unit 27	Pentecost: Whit Sunday	Acts 2:1-21	Holy Spirit
Unit 28	Trinity Sunday	2 Corinthians 13:11-13	Friends
Unit 29	All Saint's Day	Psalm 34:1-10	God's love
Unit 30	Fourth Sunday before Advent	Psalm 43	Prayer
Unit 31	Third Sunday before Advent	Psalm 70	Praise
Unit 32	Second Sunday before Advent	Psalm 90:1-8, 12	Trust
Unit 33	Christ the King	Psalm 95:1-7	Worship

SCRIPTURAL INDEX

THEMATIC INDEX

TOPIC	UNIT
Acceptance	10, 16, 23, 28
Baptism	8
Bible, the	14
Christian life	3, 9, 12, 14, 15, 17, 22, 25, 26, 27, 28, 29
Church, the	22
Death	18, 19
Decisions	15
Doubt	13, 14
Encouragement	6, 11, 22, 30, 31
Evangelism	2, 16, 21
Faith	3, 4, 5, 13, 19, 24
Forgiveness	10, 24
Generosity	28
Healing	17
Honesty	28, 30, 33
Holy Spirit, the	8, 26, 27
Gifts	7
God's love	5, 6, 8, 12, 16, 18, 20, 23, 29, 32
Jesus, life and person of	1, 3, 4, 7, 8, 11, 13, 14, 16, 19, 20, 21
Miracles	11, 18, 20
Obedience	2, 4, 5, 21, 27
Peace	21
Perseverance	24, 26, 31, 32
Possessions	23
Prayer	29, 30, 31, 32, 33
Salvation	9, 15, 20, 21, 25, 27
Serving God	11, 21, 25, 27, 29, 32
Superstition	1, 25
Trust	1, 22, 24, 25, 32
Unselfishness	23
Worry	12, 30
Worship	29, 30, 33

SIDE ORDERS

The Internet provides loads of great ideas and information on any and every topic under the sun. Finding your way around cyberspace can sometimes be similar to walking around with a bag over your head, talking on your mobile phone to a computerised answering service and listening to nursery rhymes at the same time!

To try and help you get a start, I have listed a selection of websites that you might find interesting and which will provide you with information and resources to complement the units in *Café Logos*.

Please note that websites are notorious for being 'under construction', 'we've moved' or 'no longer available'. If you cannot find or access a website use one of the many search engines available.

DRAMA
www.theworship.com/scripts/
www.dramashare.org
www.drama4church.com

ENVIRONMENT
www.christian-ecology.org.uk
www.foe.org.uk

EVENTS
www.greenbelt.org.uk
www.springh.org

HUMOUR
www.webcom.com/~ctt/comic.html
www.gospelcom.net/rev-fun/
http://ship-of-fools.com
www.funny.co.uk

MISSION
www.christiananswers.net
www.csuk.freeserve.co.uk
www.agape.org.uk

MUSIC
www.ccmcom.com
www.cnet.clara.net/links/bands.htm
www.crossrhythms.co.uk/cr/

NEWS
www.cbn.org
www.christiandailynews.org
www.churchtimes.co.uk

SEARCH
www.allinone.org
www.awesome-sites.com
www.botcw.com
www.christiantopics.com
www.goshen.net

WORSHIP
www.familyworship.org.uk
www.worship.on.ca/
www.textweek.com
www.praise.net

YOUTH
www.careforce.co.uk
www.cpas.org.uk
www.fusion.uk.com
www.everythingcool.com
www.thesite.org.uk